Envisioning Landscapes

*The Transformative
Environments of OJB*

Envisioning Landscapes

The Transformative Environments of OJB

Foreword by Christopher Hawthorne
Contributions by Peter Walker, FASLA, and Bradford McKee
Principal photography by Marion Brenner

Contents

Foreword

Christopher Hawthorne

Christopher Hawthorne is an architecture critic and the first chief design officer of the City of Los Angeles.

Duncan Martin,
Sunnylands, 2016

As the architecture critic for the *Los Angeles Times*, a job I held from 2004 to 2018, I did my best to define the position in a small-c catholic way. I wrote about architecture and design as wide-ranging and multidisciplinary subjects, with an emphasis on their role in shaping the public realm. I wrote about planning, transportation policy, the effect of immigration on the built environment, and even the ways in which architecture is represented in the movies and on television. But it was writing about landscape architecture that I found most compelling of all, for reasons that are directly reflected and easily glimpsed in the projects by OJB that fill this book.

Architecture criticism, as it has traditionally been practiced in the United States, tends to fluctuate between two poles, which might most easily be understood as the extremes of politics (or the so-called real world) on one end and formalism (or a set of inward-looking, intensely disciplinary concerns) on the other. The architecture profession itself has been similarly divided in recent decades. In landscape architecture, particularly of a type that focuses on public work or that primarily addresses the crushing realities of climate change, there is not the luxury of such choice. The sites landscape architects engage with insist on a different, less self-conscious, and, in the end, more richly productive approach. Narrow preoccupations have little room to take root in this context.

To a large extent this is because a landscape project in contemporary America begins with the need to transform or repair—to use two verbs that frame every project in this collection—a certain patch, stretch, or slice of earth. Implicit in those verbs is the notion that the site in question has been damaged, polluted, or overdeveloped or has been shaped or even deformed by a kind of overreach that needs to be reined in, softened, rethought, dismantled in order to be rebuilt or simply made whole. This is indeed the project, in a nutshell, of American urbanism in the first half of this century.

Transformation and repair become, in the designs collected here, engines for landscapes that are precise and enveloping, rigorous and welcoming, all at the same time. There is an inherent optimism in these projects, but it is kept from falling into a saccharine admiration for prettiness—or a doctrinaire insistence on well-ordered geometry for its own sake—by a frank but patient engagement with deeper issues. This begins with attention to a client's particular needs before extending to include both politics—which is to say, how cities came to look the way they do—and ecology.

Klyde Warren Park is most clearly emblematic of this sensibility in OJB's work. By spanning a sunken freeway running through the heart of Dallas, Texas, the project knits the city's ambitious Arts District, home to cultural venues by I.M. Pei, Norman Foster, Rem Koolhaas and Joshua Prince-Ramus, and Renzo Piano, among others, back into the larger urban grid. Attempts to bridge or cover stretches of freeway are not new; Lawrence Halprin's still-influential Freeway Park in Seattle opened in 1976. But in its scale and impact, Klyde Warren Park suggests that landscape architecture is capable of not only improving or revitalizing an urban district, but also thoroughly redefining its relationship to the rest of the city. Its ambition in that sense exceeds Halprin's project in Seattle.

A similarly expansive scope is clear to see in the three linked projects that OJB undertook in Oklahoma City. Including everything from elegant streetlights, botanical gardens, and fountains to public promenades and outdoor performance spaces, these interventions have helped restore residents' belief in the city's ability to deliver richly varied, well-designed, and equitable public spaces.

There are smaller gardens here, too, and more personal ones, though across the board a public-mindedness shines through. In the case of Sunnylands, where OJB teamed up with architect Frederick Fisher to turn an Annenberg family compound near Palm Springs into a visitor center and extensive garden, the restorative impulse visible in so much of the firm's work had a specific aim: to take the private residential ambition that remade Southern California across much of the twentieth century and, as if turning it inside out, remake it as an inviting civic amenity. (Sunnylands is open to the public and also frequently plays host to high-level diplomatic gatherings, extending a long-standing tradition first established in 1966, with a visit from former president Dwight D. Eisenhower.) Walter and Leonore Annenberg, in building a desert compound with the architect A. Quincy Jones in Rancho Mirage in the 1960s, famously aimed to bring the rolling green hills of their home state of Pennsylvania along with them to Southern California. To say that we understand the decision to plant grass—on or off a golf course—far differently now is an understatement. The great achievement of OJB's reimagining of these landscapes is that it trades turf and other thirsty plants for a varied palette of drought-tolerant alternatives, while meeting Mrs. Annenberg's desire for a range of lush and painterly effects.

These projects, and the others featured in the pages that follow, succeed as places for human interaction not in spite of, but thanks to their interest in precise spatial logic and sustainability. They satisfy a mixture, carefully calibrated, of social, formal, urban, and planetary goals. They also interact superbly with architecture. (A separate essay could be written on the complementary relationship between OJB's work and that of Fisher, Thomas Phifer, and the firm's other regular collaborators.) Few landscape practices I can think of blend these priorities so subtly or effectively. Fewer still turn them to the pressing work of reparative, transformative design with such consistent, even-keeled sophistication.

The Landscape Art of James Burnett

Peter Walker, FASLA

Peter Walker is an internationally recognized landscape architect and founder of PWP Landscape Architecture

Duncan Martin, *Brochstein Pavilion, Rice University*, 2010

This monograph on the work of OJB—known during its first decades as the Office of James Burnett—comes as a particular pleasure for me because when I first met Jim in 1984 through our mutual friend, the late architect Paul Kennon, Jim was considering switching to a career in architecture. Happily for us all, he continued in landscape architecture and produced the distinguished body of work that is displayed here. Over the years, I have watched these projects develop and have had the pleasure of spending time in a number of them.

For 150 years, American gardens and parks were influenced by English naturalism and European formalism, which gave way in the second half of the twentieth century to function-based modernism in architecture and then landscape. In the last twenty years, modernism has expanded to include ecological determinism. Jim has been keenly aware of these historic movements, and we can feel their synthesized influence in his designs, which make a powerful argument for the enrichment of open spaces in today's automobile-dominated cities.

Landscape design is perhaps the most difficult of the environmental arts because it relies on living material and, therefore, is dependent on the designer's powers of prediction. Each of us develops work that can only succeed over time, based at least partly on our ability to predict the changing growth that brings it to aesthetic and functional fruition. This realization of our work is also contingent on the care that it receives over its lifetime, particularly in its early formative years. Every project must express and maintain cultural value in order to gain the participation of its original client and then its subsequent owners.

In this monograph, a selection of OJB's projects covering a wide range of urban and institutional examples developed over the last thirty-two years is explained visually with vivid photographs. Frequently a project features a large,

sweeping pathway or a shaded promenade that directs the visitor's attention both left and right and ties together a wide variety of special-use gardens, such as open greens, children's play areas, plant and botanic displays, and spaces for indoor and outdoor dining, all in an array of scales and degrees of visual richness. Pedestrians entering from various directions encounter a series of unique gardens. Aerial photographs reveal the projects' relationships with specific parts of the surrounding city, campus, or corporate institution.

One of the most distinctive elements of Jim's work is the diversity of complex plantings, from shade trees to rich groundcover, and surprising plant combinations not seen in most of today's designed public open spaces. OJB has continuously explored a wide range of plant relationships over the projects shown here, and the office's use of plant combinations is among the very best of those practicing in the field today. Although there are a number of interesting collaborations by landscape architects and plant experts (one thinks of New York's Highline and Chicago's Lurie Garden), many require annual replanting and extensive maintenance; OJB's projects, by contrast, are planted to allow the landscapes to transform and mature over time.

In addition to a rich plant palette, the gardens show a consistent bravery in the development of bold plant and construction material, giving each project an original expression linked to its specific region and subtly but intentionally setting them apart from one another.

Although Jim has continued to practice landscape architecture, he has maintained a particularly refined sense of landscape-related public architecture. The structures in his parks and gardens, designed by many important architects, are both memorable and restrained. These landscapes do not merely extend the interior of the structures, but more often complement and contrast their built elegance with a rich garden elegance. I particularly appreciate the handling of performance areas made of a sophisticated blending of classically modern structure and visually memorable landscape with a myriad of textures, areas of light and shade, and contrasting colors, while still remaining strongly spatial. These landscapes contain inventive compositions in form and scale, both orthogonal and biomorphic. Water often has an important role, from cool reflecting surfaces to exuberant explosions encouraging physical play.

The modern practice of programming the specific uses of carefully designed spaces is deployed by OJB in most of their work. For instance, consider the grandeur of Dallas's Klyde Warren Park—a deck park built over a busy freeway—which joins previously disconnected parts of the city while providing a new destination of recreation areas, performance spaces, and greatly expanded public dining facilities for both the Arts District and Uptown, neighborhoods that had been cut off by the freeway. If we remember the barren expanse of concrete that existed on the site before and that provided only noise and air pollution, we can appreciate the miraculous transformation.

Sunnylands Center and Gardens in Rancho Mirage offers an example of the opposite end of the urban scale. Small, intimate, and protected, this garden provides a private sanctuary for conversation and quiet contemplation—a lovely retreat from daily life in a hectic world. Here, quiet reigns.

This book is as useful as it is beautiful. At the end of each project a concise analysis addresses its specific environmental solutions. These outlines inform the reader, and especially the student, of the complex goals that modern designed landscapes can and do strive for in economic, environmental, social, and physical realms. This book is an important exposition of joyfully sustainable public landscape art.

Rethinking the Public Realm

Klyde Warren Park

Dallas, Texas

The park has transformed the city by reconnecting Dallas's two largest cultural districts and creating a new heart for downtown.

Klyde Warren Park was created over one of the busiest freeways in Texas through a creative visioning process and public-private partnership. The freeway had severed Dallas's two largest cultural districts—the downtown Arts District and Uptown—for many years. Restoring the connection by bridging the gap has transformed the city and made a new heart for downtown.

Bisected by the existing Olive Street Bridge, the 5.2-acre park is organized around a sweeping pedestrian promenade shaded by a continuous canopy of specimen pond cypress. The promenade draws visitors through the park past a botanical garden, a reading room, an event lawn, and a children's garden with an interactive water feature. A large public plaza adjacent to Olive Street also includes an interactive fountain and connects a restaurant terrace, a performance pavilion, and a casual takeout kiosk to the street . A series of arches establish a strong architectural rhythm through the park, and groves of trees buffer the interior spaces from the busy adjacent surface streets.

The park contributes to a sense of place that is otherwise lacking in the city's core. It incorporates many of the area's most prominent museums and universities in its programming and places them in an environment featuring a palette of regionally appropriate trees, shrubs, and ornamental plantings—of which over 50 percent are native to the North Texas area. Klyde Warren Park brings people together in new ways, with dozens of free activities and amenities on offer, from concerts and lectures to games and fitness classes, all within a five-acre composition.

The performance pavilion anchors
the great lawn on the west side
and shades the adjacent children's
water plaza on the east.

In the children's park, programmed jets
bring water and cooling mist into the play
environment. Rolling berms wrapped in
turf are shaded by a grove of river birch.

↑   8 November | 2:19 p.m.
→   16 June | 7:44 p.m.

↑ Groves of trees and arched structures
establish a strong architectural rhythm along
the promenade. → Food trucks provided a
temporary food option during restaurant
construction and were so popular that they
became a permanent feature.

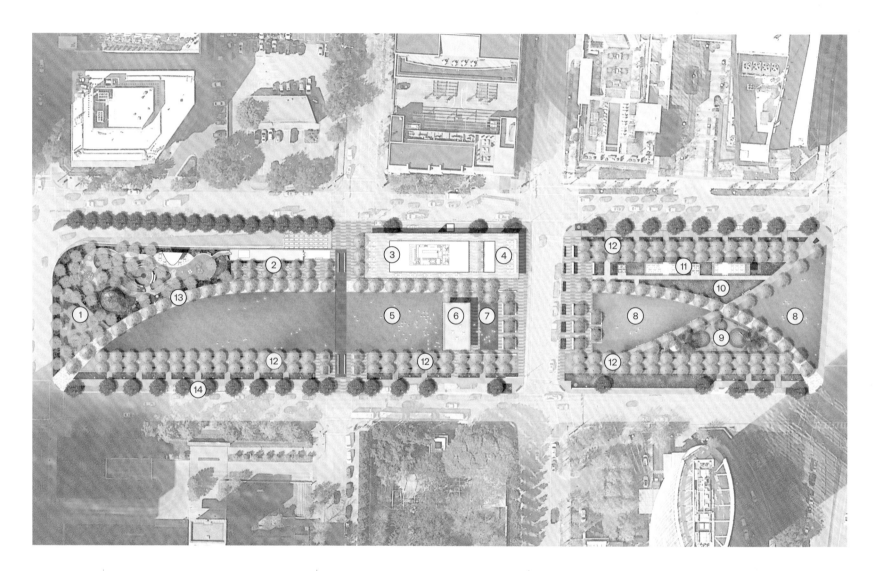

1. Children's park
2. Reading room
3. Restaurant
4. Food and beverage kiosk
5. Great lawn
6. Performance pavilion
7. Water feature plaza
8. East lawn
9. Dog park
10. Botanical garden
11. Game pavilions
12. Pedestrian streetscape
13. Promenade
14. Food trucks

Plantings

TREES

Betula nigra 'Dura Heat', river birch

Pistacia chinensis, Chinese pistache

Quercus macrocarpa, bur oak

Quercus shumardii, shumard oak

Quercus virginiana 'Cathedral', cathedral live oak

Taxodium ascendens, pond cypress

Ulmus parvifolia 'Allee', lacebark elm

SHRUBS

Agave havardiana, Havard's century plant

Agave lophantha, thorn-crested agave

Agave × 'Mr. Ripple', Mr. Ripple agave

Agave toumeyana var. *bella*, miniature century plant

Hesperaloe parviflora, red yucca

Leucophyllum frutescens, Del Rio Texas sage/cenizo

Myrica cerifera, wax myrtle

Salvia leucantha, Mexican bush sage

Yucca arkansana, Arkansas yucca

PERENNIALS

Achillea millefolium, yarrow

Aster oblongifolius, fall aster

Coreopsis grandiflora, large-flowered tickseed

Dietes iridioides, African iris

Echinacea purpurea, purple coneflower

Equisetum hyemale, horsetail

Eupatorium greggii, West Texas mist flower

Lantana montevidensis, trailing lantana

Liatris spicata, blazing star

Melampodium leucanthum, blackfoot daisy

Perovskia atriplicifolia, Russian sage

Phlox pilosa, prairie phlox

Physostegia virginiana, obedient plant

Rudbeckia fulgida, black-eyed Susan

Salvia farinacea, mealy blue sage

Salvia greggii, Gregg's salvia

Scutellaria suffrutescens, Texas skullcap

Verbena bipinnatifida, prairie verbena

GRASSES

Andropogon virginicus, broomsedge bluestem

Eragrostis curvula, weeping lovegrass

Miscanthus sinensis, silver grass

Miscanthus sinensis 'Adagio', adagio silver grass

Muhlenbergia capillaris, gulf muhly

Muhlenbergia lindheimeri, Lindheimer muhly

Muhlenbergia reverchonii, seep muhly

Nassella tenuissima, Mexican feathergrass

Poa arachnifera, Texas bluegrass

Setaria scheelei, southwestern bristlegrass

Sorghastrum nutans, Indian grass

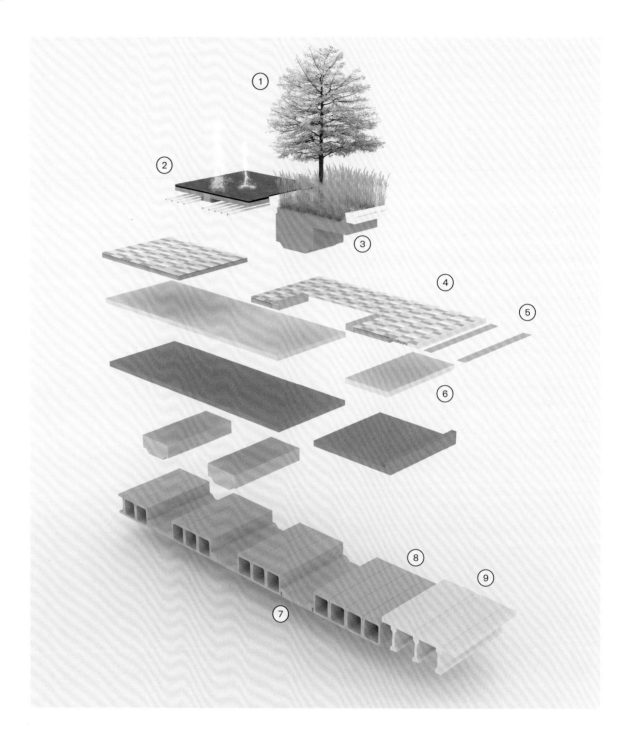

1. Regionally appropriate plants
2. Amenity features
3. Engineered soil
4. Pedestrian paving system
5. Light-rail track
6. Engineered structural fill
7. Drop slab inserts
8. Prestressed box beam system
9. Existing bridge structure

Sustainability

LAND

300 prestressed box beams

5 feet of fill and 18 inches of soil

200-foot stretch of freeway concealed

WATER

50% permeability increase

12,000 gallons of gray water collected in the reservoir for irrigation

64,214 gallons of stormwater runoff can be intercepted annually by new tree canopies*

Excess water stored in drainage mat between soil and deck infrastructure

PLANTING

322 trees, 904 shrubs, 3,292 perennials

52% native to North Texas

CARBON, ENERGY & AIR

LED lighting fixtures

Geothermal energy for heating and cooling the restaurant

18,500 pounds of carbon—equivalent to emissions produced by driving 22,636 miles in a passenger vehicle—sequestered annually by newly planted trees**

ECONOMICS

32% increase in lease rates at Trammell Crow Center

46% increase in lease rates at 2100 Ross

56% increase in lease rates at 2000 McKinney

$11,200 annual savings through LED lighting

$312.7 million in economic development and $12.7 million in tax revenue projected

8.8% population increase projected in the two Census Block Groups surrounding the park as a result of development spurred by the park, supporting the regional goal of making metropolitan centers attractive and livable

SOCIAL

15 programmed spaces

48 tables, 374 chairs for visitors

5.2-acre park adds .5 miles of walkable streetscapes and 9 crosswalks

2 million visitors hosted during first two years

Contributed to 61% increase in ridership on public transportation connecting downtown Arts District and Uptown and led to three new stops adjacent to the park

14,683 "likes," and 5,212 tagged photos on Facebook, 6,890 Twitter followers, and 959 Instagram followers in first six months indicate social interaction beyond park boundaries

Levy Park

Houston, Texas

This project remakes a forty-year-old park in Houston to provide better public access and address flooding issues. With only a single entrance point and private development surrounding the site, Levy Park suffered from low patronage over the course of its history. Restoring access to and activating this urban park were the foundation of its transformation.

A public-private partnership allowed for a complete reexamination of the site. Adjacent development parcels were assembled to the east and northeast, opening access to a major thoroughfare. By incorporating park roads on the north and south borders of the project, the design solved access, visibility, and circulation problems inhibiting activation and strengthened pedestrian and vehicular connectivity.

High visibility into the park from the street signals openness and activity, and multiple access points lead visitors directly to the main social gathering areas. There, a diverse collection of programmed spaces includes an activity lawn; a gaming area with a shade arbor where parkgoers can play checkers, foosball, ping-pong, or miniature golf; a large gated children's garden designed to spark the imagination; a reading room; small and large dog play

areas with berms and water features that keep dogs cool and hydrated; and a lively community garden. A multipurpose performance pavilion looks out onto an event lawn that can seat three thousand, welcoming the downtown neighborhood back into the park. Encircling the entire green space is a generous promenade.

The children's garden is at the heart of the park and features a 150-foot-long tree house that rises at an ADA-accessible grade and is wrapped around relocated forty- to seventy-year-old legacy live oak trees. The generous tree canopy provides protection from the sun and, from the tree house, thrilling views of the park areas below. The sizable play area also offers plenty of other opportunities for fun. Children can climb a rock wall, slide down a seven-foot-wide slide, crawl through LED-lit tunnels, and dance in a three-tiered interactive water feature that mimics a Houston rain shower.

Climate resiliency is essential to the park's design. To mitigate Houston's heat, humidity, and frequent flooding, the project features 3.3 acres of permeable surface, together with multiple strategies for stormwater control. The 7,500-square-foot rain garden and the community garden both harvest and reuse stormwater. Intercepting 80,000 gallons of stormwater runoff are 138 new native trees, which also provide shade to park-goers. The magnificent new canopy created by preserving and relocating the legacy live oaks offers further protection from the elements and reduces temperatures in the park by an estimated ten degrees.

A diverse collection of high visibility and lively programmed spaces bring the neighborhood back into the park.

A pavilion greets visitors at the entry to the park and frames the event lawn. This structure is a flexible backdrop for a wide range of community events.

← 2 June | 8:30 p.m.

Large live oak trees, plenty of movable
furniture, and benches surrounding
planted berms help to define a series of
outdoor rooms near the pavilion.

← 13 October | 10:25 a.m.
↑ 13 October | 11:39 a.m.

↑ 2 June | 8:19 p.m.

← A winding path just below the tree canopy is imagined as an elevated tree house. ↑ The children's play areas are filled with active elements—tunnels, slides, water features, and musical sculptures.

→ At the entries into the park, visitors are greeted with a rich array of textures and colors.

← 14 October | 2:06 p.m.

← Rain gardens in the park collect and reuse stormwater, creatively mitigating Houston's frequent rain showers. → In the dog park, play berms and water fountains keep dogs entertained, cool, and hydrated.

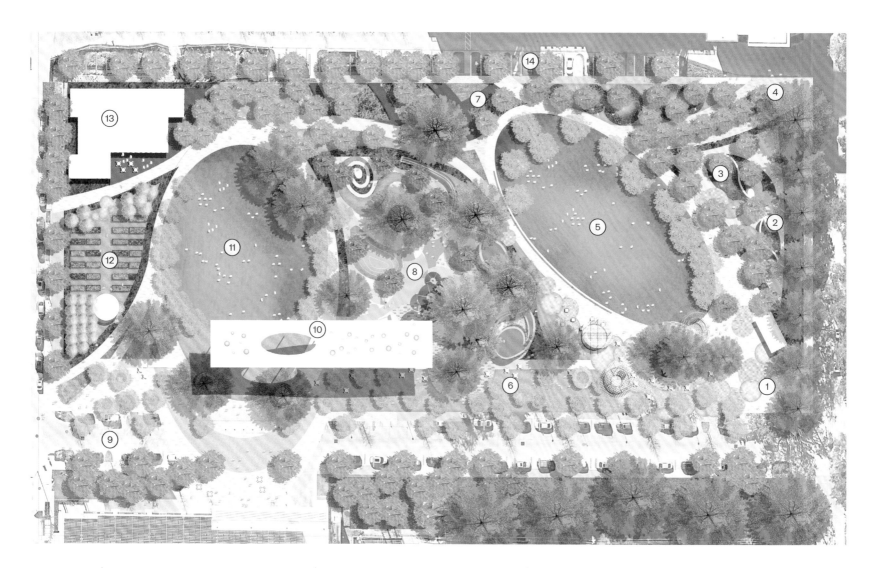

1. Welcome entry and café
2. Small dog park
3. Large dog park
4. Welcome entry
5. Activity lawn

6. Seating grove
7. Rain garden
8. Structured children's play
9. Entry plaza
10. Performance pavilion

11. Event lawn
12. Community garden
13. Café and dining terrace
14. Parking

Plantings

TREES

Citrus × meyeri, Meyer lemon

Citrus unshiu, satsuma orange

Quercus lyrata, overcup oak

Quercus virginiana, live oak

Taxodium ascendens, pond cypress

Taxodium distichum, bald cypress

Ulmus parvifolia 'Emer II', Allee lacebark elm

SHRUBS & GROUNDCOVER

Acca sellowiana, pineapple guava

Asparagus aethiopicus, foxtail fern

Carex cherokeensis, Cherokee sedge

Chasmanthium latifolium, inland sea oats

Cyperus alternifolius, umbrella plant

Dianella tasmanica, flax lily

Eleocharis montevidensis, sand spikerush

Ficus pumila, fig ivy

Ficus tikoua, sandyleaf fig ivy

Iris pseudacorus, yellow flag iris

Iris spuria, butterfly iris

Itea virginica, Virginia sweetspire

Ligularia tussilaginea 'Gigantea', giant ligularia

Lycoris radiata, spider lily

Miscanthus sinensis 'Morning Light', Morning Light miscanthus

Myrica cerifera, wax myrtle

Nephrolepis biserrata 'Macho', Macho fern

Phyla nodiflora, frogfruit

Pontederia cordata, pickerelweed

Rudbeckia hirta, black-eyed Susan

Sabal minor, dwarf palmetto

Salvia leucantha, Mexican bush sage

Sphagneticola trilobata, wedelia

Trachelospermum asiaticum, Asian jasmine

LAWN

Cynodon dactylon, Bermuda grass

Sustainability

LAND

Floodplain function protected by design

Partially degraded site restored

WATER

7,500-square-foot detention garden manages stormwater while acting as amenity

Employs land mitigation strategy and meets Houston detention requirement

80,000 gallons of stormwater runoff—equivalent to the daily water usage of 800 Americans—can be intercepted annually by trees*

3.3 acres of permeable surface created

PLANTING

Vegetation conserved by saving and transplanting trees on-site

20 trees protected and 9 large trees with diameters of 36–48 inches in caliper relocated

138 trees planted

84,787 square feet of planting

32% native species

CARBON, ENERGY & AIR

10-degree decrease in temperatures in the park due to tree canopy

19,200 pounds of carbon sequestered annually by trees**

Pollutants controlled and retained during construction

ECONOMICS

170% increase in property values (from $81 to $140 per square foot) to the west and 200% increase (from $46 to $92 per square foot) to the north

SOCIAL

Active and lively Urban Harvest community garden hosted by the park

Existing gardens enhanced through design

Pop-up farmers market accommodated by parking lot design

The park is highly programmed and features a restaurant, activity lawn, dog park, playground, rain garden, and educational and fitness facilities for the community

Oklahoma City Renaissance

Oklahoma City, Oklahoma

Completed over a five-year period, three interwoven projects—the Devon Energy landscape, the Myriad Botanical Gardens renovation, and the revitalization of nearby streets—transformed downtown Oklahoma City into an integrated public realm of streets, parks, and open spaces. The newly built Devon Energy headquarters and the building's connection to the street edge prompted this large-scale activation. An open 2.25-acre public space acts as a foreground for the building podium, winter garden, and tower and includes an informal dining terrace punctuated by a series of pools and a public green that can accommodate two thousand people. At the western edge of the lawn, a pavilion rises from a skin of water and provides a space for special events. Along the northern edge, planting and fountain features insulate private courtyards from the noise and activity of the park.

While development of the landscape was underway, a concurrent study of the streetscape in the district led to a public-private partnership focused on replanning downtown streets and parking to calm traffic and return trees and landscape to the pedestrian experience. Nearly eight miles of streets were updated with new intersections, pavement, site amenities, street trees, and abundant on-street parking, making the downtown more walkable.

Spurred by the encouraging changes within the 180 acres of the downtown core, including the alignment of seventeen streets, the OJB team was engaged to renovate fifteen acres of quiet, underutilized open space at Myriad Botanical Gardens, the downtown core's major public amenity. Rethinking how to activate the space led to the creation of a series of interconnected public plazas, courtyards, and gardens that are flexible, functional, and attractive year-round. Since its reopening in 2011, the park has welcomed more than a million visitors annually and catalyzed downtown economic development, earning it an Urban Land Institute Urban Open Space Award.

Three interwoven projects transformed downtown Oklahoma City into an integrated public realm of streets, parks, and open spaces.

Myriad Botanical Gardens

Myriad Botanical Gardens was long envisioned as the cultural heart of the downtown core. The Crystal Bridge Conservatory opened to the public in 1985, and the gardens slowly grew by accretion, although the vision for the site was never fully realized. A new socially enriched concept for open space was made possible by rethinking access, program, and permeability. The public-private partnership that enabled the redesign was funded by TIF district proceeds from the construction of the adjacent Devon Energy headquarters.

← 26 May | 2:03 p.m.
→ 26 May | 1:27 p.m.

← At the entry to the children's garden, an interactive water feature simulates an Oklahoma thunderstorm.
↑ Water features and children's play areas are essential to the garden's community appeal.

← 14 July | 06:30 p.m.

↑ A water feature transforms from an ice rink into a reflecting pool, encouraging social gathering throughout the seasons. → Water is circulated throughout the park's pools and garden areas. A terraced botanical garden offers a more contemplative experience adjacent to the pond.

Devon Energy

The Devon Energy tower is an urban office campus in the heart of downtown Oklahoma City. The company's focus on publicly accessible gardens expresses a corporate culture that embraces health and wellness.

The perimeter streetscape along West Sheridan Avenue is graced with canopy shade trees and gardens.

Streetscape 180

This comprehensive design approach to the urban realm includes narrowing and eliminating one-way streets, adding new street trees, understory planting, LED lighting, wayfinding, street furnishings, and public art, and implementing integrated streetscape standards throughout the central core.

A new visual language is deployed throughout the city, with generous sidewalks framed by layered planting and anchored by street trees. The trees contribute many benefits, including lowering surface temperatures, absorbing pollutants, and encouraging walkability throughout the downtown core.

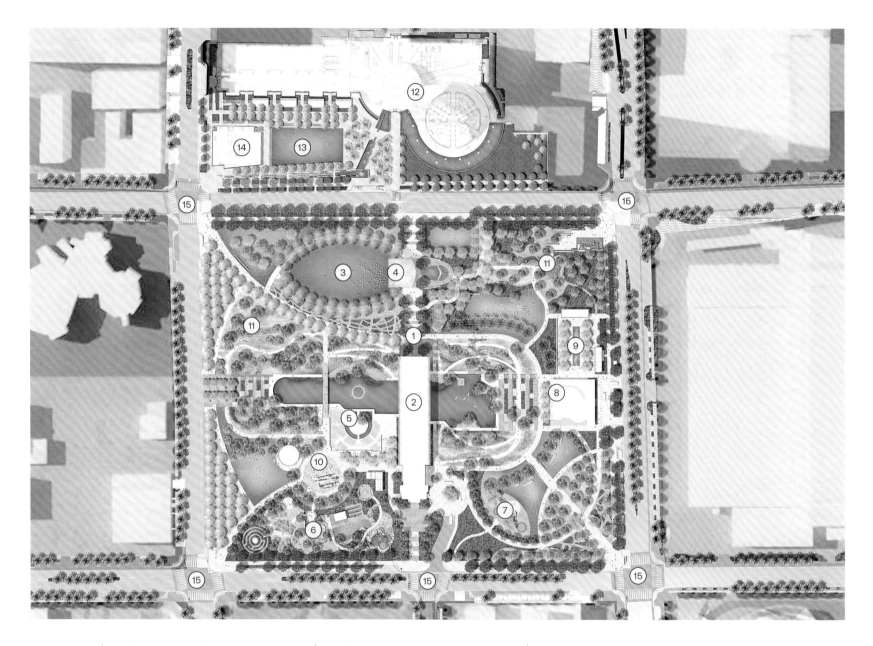

1. Myriad Botanical Gardens
2. Crystal Bridge Conservatory
3. Performance lawn
4. Band shell
5. Amphitheater

6. Children's garden
7. Dog park
8. Restaurant
9. Seasonal plaza
10. Fountain plaza

11. Specialty gardens
12. Devon Energy headquarters
13. Event lawn
14. Pavilion
15. Streetscape 180 improvements

Plantings – Devon Energy

TREES

Gleditsia triacanthos 'Shade Master', Shade Master honey locust

Phyllostachys decora, beautiful bamboo

Quercus muehlenbergii, chinquapin oak

Quercus shumardii, shumard oak

Ulmus parvifolia, lacebark elm

SHRUBS, PERENNIALS, GRASSES & GROUNDCOVERS

Athyrium 'Ghost', lady fern

Crocosmia 'Vulcan', montbretia

Cornus sericea 'Kelseyi', dwarf red-twig dogwood

Equisetum hyemale, horsetail

Geranium macrorrhizum, bigroot cranesbill

Iris sibirica, Siberian iris

Liatris spicata 'Floristan White', white liatris

Liatris spicata 'Purple', blazing star

Liriope muscari 'Majestic', lilyturf

Miscanthus sinensis 'Yaku Jima', dwarf maiden grass

Nepeta faassenii 'Six Hills Giant', Six Hills giant catmint

Pennisetum alopecuroides 'Cassian', fountain grass

Salvia yangii, Russian sage

Parthenocissus tricuspidata 'Fenway Park', Boston ivy

Spiraea × bumalda 'Anthony Waterer', Anthony Waterer spirea

Taxus × media 'Runyan', Runyan yew

Tricyrtis hirta, hairy toad lily

Narcissus 'Tahiti', Tahiti daffodil

Plantings – Myriad Botanical Gardens

TREES

Acer truncatum, shantung maple

Carpinus betulus, European hornbeam

Cupressus arizonica var. *glabra* 'Blue Pyramid', Blue Pyramid cypress

Diospyros virginiana, persimmon

Koelreuteria paniculata, golden rain tree

Lagerstroemia indica × fauriei 'Natchez', Natchez crape myrtle

Magnolia grandiflora, southern magnolia

Malus 'Spring Snow', spring snow crabapple

Pistacia chinensis, Chinese pistache

Platanus occidentalis, sycamore

Taxodium ascendens, pond cypress

Quercus macrocarpa, bur oak

Quercus shumardii, shumard oak

SHRUBS

Agave parryi, Parry's agave

Agave parryi var. *truncata*, artichoke agave

Amorpha fruticosa, desert false indigo

Amorpha canescens, lead plant

Amorphophallus konjac, devil's tongue

Bignonia capreolata, cross vine

Buxus, boxwood

Buddleja davidii, butterfly bush

Callicarpa americana, American beautyberry

Caryopteris × clandonensis, blue mist shrub

Ceanothus americanus, New Jersey tea

Cephalanthus occidentalis, common buttonbush

Clematis vitalba, evergreen clematis

Clethra alnifolia, summersweet clethra

Cornus alba 'Sibirica', red-twig dogwood

Cornus sericea 'Flaviramea', yellow-twig dogwood

Euonymus americanus, strawberry bush

Euonymus fortunei 'Coloratus', purple wintercreeper

Bambusa vulgaris, bamboo

Fothergilla gardenii, dwarf fothergilla

Hamamelis virginiana, American witch hazel

Hibiscus moscheutos, hardy hibiscus

Hydrangea arborescens 'Annabelle', Annabelle hydrangea

Hydrangea quercifolia, oakleaf hydrangea

Ilex glabra, inkberry

Ilex vomitoria 'Nana', dwarf yaupon holly

Itea virginica, Virginia sweetspire

Itea virginica 'Little Henry', Little Henry Virginia sweetspire

Juniperus conferta, shore juniper

Juniperus squamata 'Blue Star', Blue Star juniper

Lagerstroemia indica, crape myrtle

Lavandula × intermedia, lavandin

Lindera benzoin, northern spicebush

Parthenocissus quinquefolia, Virginia creeper

Physocarpus opulifolius, common ninebark

Pinus mugo, mountain pine

Prunus angustifolia, chickasaw plum

Phyllostachys nigra, black bamboo

Rhododendron 'Abbey's Re-View', hybrid rhododendron

Rhododendron sp., azalea hybrid

Rhododendron 'Robleg' Autumn Angel, Encore Autumn Angel azalea

Rhododendron viscosum, swamp azalea

Rhus aromatica 'Gro-Low', fragrant sumac

Rhus glabra, smooth sumac

Ribes odoratum 'Crandall', clove currant

Rosa arkansana, prairie rose

Rosa 'Radwhite', White Out rose

Salvia leucantha, Mexican brush sage

Sambucus nigra ssp. canadensis, common elderberry

Spiraea japonica, Japanese spirea

Taxus × media 'Taunton', Taunton yew

Viburnum carlesii 'Compactum', Korean spice viburnumw

Viburnum × burkwoodii, burkwood viburnum

Yucca filamentosa, spoonleaf yucca

PERENNIALS

Achillea filipendulina 'Coronation Gold', fern-leaf yarrow

Adiantum capillus-veneris, southern maidenhair fern

Adiantum pedatum, northern maidenhair fern

Agastache aurantiaca 'Shades of Orange', Shades of Orange hummingbird mint

Artemisia 'Powis Castle', wormwood

Asclepias tuberosa, butterfly milkweed

Baptisia 'Carolina Moonlight', false indigo

Callirhoe involucrata, purple poppy mallow

Coreopsis grandiflora, large-flowered tickseed

Coreopsis lanceolata, lanceleaf coreopsis

Dryopteris marginalis, marginal wood fern

Eryngium × zabelii 'Big Blue', sea holly

Echinacea pallida, pale purple coneflower

Echinacea paradoxa, yellow coneflower

Echinops ritro, southern globe thistle

Equisetum arvense, rough horsetail

Eutrochium purpureum, sweet-scented joepye-weed

Euphorbia cyparissias, cypress Spurge

Fragaria virginiana, scarlet strawberry

Geranium maculatum 'Espresso', spotted geranium

Hemerocallis 'Summer Interlude', Summer Interlude daylily

Hosta 'Krossa Regal', hosta

Hosta 'Sum & Substance', hosta

Iris virginica 'Contraband Girl', southern blue flag iris

Kniphofia uvaria, grass-leaf red-hot poker

Liatris pycnostachya, prairie blazing star

Liriope spicata, creeping lily turf

Lobelia cardinalis, cardinal flower

Monarda fistulosa, wild bergamot

Nepeta × faassenii, Faassen's catmint

Osmundastrum cinnamomeum, cinnamon fern

Osmunda regalis, royal fern

Salvia yangii, Russian sage

Phlox divaricate, wild blue phlox

Physostegia virginiana, obedient plant

Polystichum acrostichoides, Christmas fern

Rudbeckia maxima, great coneflower

Salvia nemorosa 'Rosenwein', rose wine sage

Salvia × sylvestris 'Blue Hill', Blue Hill meadow sage

Santolina rosmarinifolia, green santolina

Solidago, dwarf goldenrod

Stachys byzantina, lamb's ear

Verbena bonariensis, purple verbena

AQUATIC PLANTS

Acorus gramineus, Japanese rush

Arisaema triphyllum, jack-in-the-pulpit

Canna indica, canna lily

Carex flacca, blue sedge

Colocasia esculenta, taro

Iris pseudacorus 'Variegata', variegated yellow flag

Justicia americana, American water willow

Juncus effusus, rush

Nelumbo lutea, American lotus

Nymphaea odorata, white water lily

Peltandra virginica, green arrow arum

Pontederia cordata, pickerel weed

Thalia dealbata, powdery thalia

GRASSES

Calamagrostis 'Karl Foerster', feather reed grass

Carex aquatilis, water sedge

Carex laxiculmis 'Hobb', bunny blue sedge

Carex testacea, orange New Zealand sedge

Chasmanthium latifolium, Indian woodoats

Eragrostis curvula, weeping lovegrass

Festuca glauca, blue fescue

Hakonechloa macra 'Nicolas', Japanese forest grass

Helictotrichon sempervirens, blue oat grass

Leymus arenarius 'Blue Dune', blue lyme grass

Miscanthus sinensis, maiden grass

Muhlenbergia capillaris, pink muhlygrass

Nassella tenuissima, Mexican feather grass

Pennisetum alopecuroides 'Hameln', dwarf fountain grass

Schizachyrium scoparium 'The Blues', little bluestem grass

Sesleria autumnalis, autumn moor grass

Sisyrinchium angustifolium, narrowleaf blue-eyed grass

Sorghastrum nutans 'Indian Steel', Indian grass

Sustainability – Myriad Botanical Gardens

LAND

15-acre gardens restored and enhanced to celebrate natural beauty of indigenous landscape

Historic context of site enhanced through renovations of Crystal Bridge Conservatory

Visitors encouraged to enter park by removal of high perimeter berm

Erosion controlled by soil-stabilizing geotextiles and retaining walls that divert water

WATER

3-acre central lake fed by groundwater

Rainfall captured in storm system directed to existing lake, then reused for water features and irrigation

85% of surfaces permeable

Water quality of existing lake improved, turbidity decreased, and temperature regulated by dredging, cleaning, and creation of biofiltration system to support a healthy ecosystem

16,900 gallons of water—equivalent to the daily water usage of 1,690 Americans—can be intercepted annually by trees*

PLANTING

300 existing trees preserved

380 trees planted

25 high-value specimen and several trees with diameters of 16–24 inches in caliper transplanted on-site

Pollinators supported by butterfly garden in children's play area and prairie garden at entry

Increased water and nutrient absorption by planting promoted through mycorrhizal fungi implemented in soil mix; carbohydrates for fungi provided, in turn, by planting

Lake naturally maintained through vegetated wetland planters, which also add aesthetic beauty

CARBON, ENERGY & AIR

Regional material such as locally sourced stone and gravel utilized, reducing emissions resulting from transportation

Park temperatures reduced and energy cost savings generated from tree canopy

81,600 pounds of carbon—equivalent to emissions produced by driving 111,003 miles in a passenger vehicle—sequestered annually by trees**

ECONOMICS

Property values increased due to park's restoration

Maintenance savings achieved due to design strategy

SOCIAL

Jobs created and local economy boosted by site, which attracts 1,000,000 visitors annually

Programmed spaces with daily events, including 6,500-square-foot dog park, 10,500-square-foot seasonal plaza, 28,000-square-foot event lawn, 9,400-square-foot activity lawn, 35,000-square-foot children's garden, arena plaza, restaurant, café, groves, arts plaza, and botanical garden, draw visitors

Educational signage about plants, place, and ecology installed throughout park

Wireless network free on-site

The Park at
Lakeshore East

Chicago, Illinois

At the confluence of the Chicago River and Lake Michigan, the park anchors a livable downtown district.

Prominently sited at the confluence of the Chicago River and Lake Michigan, this twenty-eight-acre development in the Loop was one of the last open parcels in the city. In consideration of the scale of its mixed-use program, which includes 4,950 residential units, 1,500 hotel rooms, 2.2 million gross square feet of commercial space, 770,000 square feet of retail space, and an elementary school, all anchored by an urban park as the central amenity, a strong, geometric organizational language with curving elements at the street scale was deployed. The main component connecting the site to the river and the lakefront, the 5.3-acre park is notable for turning the edge of the city into a destination in itself and establishing a new livable downtown district.

At the southern park entry, a grand staircase addresses a significant grade change across the site and creates an overlook terrace with expansive views into the park. The northern entry is marked by long seating walls, a strong geometric pavement pattern, and sequenced landscape plantings that evolve into serene open spaces. Families of site furnishings and lighting, pavement in a variety of materials and colors, and the rich variation of Lannon Stone, granite, cedar wood, and metals meld into a contemporary composition that provides a distinctive material vocabulary throughout.

From the raised roadways, including the realigned Lake Shore Drive, the park appears as a "town square" for the new residential district, a vibrant patch of green surrounded by towers and spanned by the sail-like forms of the arcing main park promenades. These two paths, constructed of specialty pavement, are the primary circulation across the site and establish the eastern and western entry terraces. Visitors entering the park at each terrace are met by a sequence of five pools separated by fields of decomposed granite and punctuated by specimen shade trees. In keeping with the park's character as a passive neighborhood space, the water features are contemplative: each basin is lined with rugged basalt boulders to provide a deep, richly textured water surface and continuous interest when the fountains are dormant for the winter months.

A dog park, with circular calming entry points and sculpted landforms for play, and three play pods in a large children's playground are the active areas that strike a balance with the passive park features.

← 25 September | 10:33 a.m.
→ 19 April | 10:34 a.m.

↑ Gentle topography creates a
playground for dogs at the park.

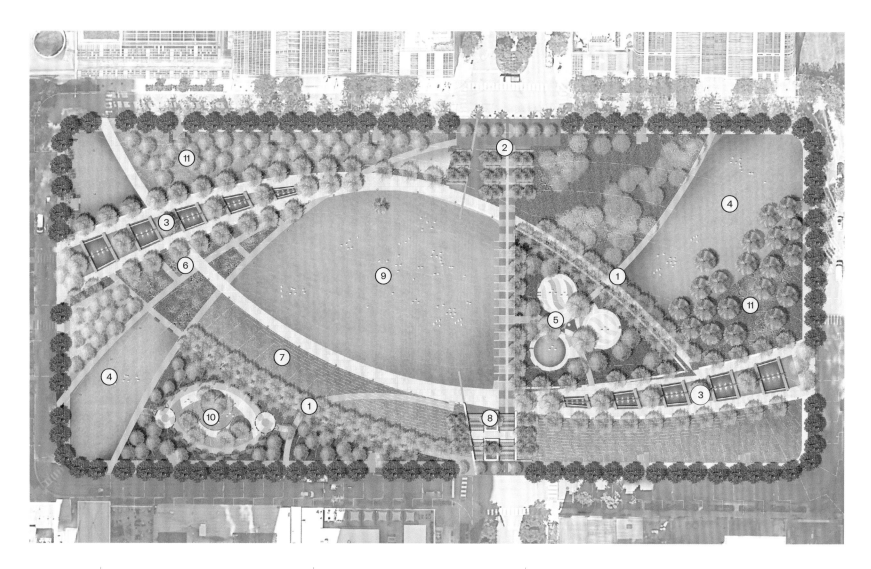

1. Promenade
2. Entry plaza
3. Water garden
4. Activity lawn

5. Children's play garden
6. Botanical garden
7. Hillside
8. Grand stair

9. Open space
10. Dog park
11. Grove

Plantings

TREES

Abies concolor, white fir

Amelanchier × grandiflora 'Autumn Brilliance', apple serviceberry

Betula nigra, river birch

Cercis canadensis, eastern redbud

Gleditsia triacanthos var. *inermis* 'Skyline', Skyline honey locust

Malus transitoria 'Golden Raindrops', Golden Raindrops crabapple

Metasequoia, dawn redwood

Pinus nigra, Austrian pine

Platanus × acerifolia, London plane tree

Pseudotsuga menziesii, Douglas fir

Pyrus calleryana 'Cleveland Select', Cleveland select Bradford pear

Quercus bicolor, swamp white oak

Quercus ellipsoidalis, northern pin oak

Ulmus 'Homestead', Homestead elm

Ulmus 'Morton', Accolade elm

SHRUBS

Buxus × 'Glencoe', Chicagoland Green boxwood

Cornus sericea 'Isanti', Isanti red-twig dogwood

Hesperaloe parviflora, red yucca

Leucophyllum frutescens, Texas sage

Myrica cerifera, wax myrtle

Rosa 'Bucbi', Carefree Beauty rose

Rosa 'Meicoublan', White Meidiland rose

Rosa 'Meipitac', Carefree Wonder rose

Rosa 'Nearly Wild', Nearly Wild rose

Rosa 'Poulemb', Cliffs of Dover rose

Syringa pubescens subsp. *patula* 'Miss Kim', Miss Kim lilac

Taxus × media 'Densiformis', dense yew

PERENNIALS & GRASSES

Achillea 'Moonshine', yarrow

Artemisia schmidtiana, silver mound

Baptisia australis, blue wild indigo

Buddleja davidii, butterfly bush

Buddleja davidii 'White Profusion', white butterfly bush

Calamagrostis × acutiflora, feather reed grass

Cenchrus setaceus, fountain grass

Dianthus gratianapolitanus 'Firewitch', Firewitch pinks

Echinacea purpurea magnus, Magnus purple coneflower

Helictotrichon sempervirens, blue oat grass

Hemerocallis 'Barbara Mitchell', Barbara Mitchell daylily

Hemerocallis 'Chicago Royal Robe', Chicago Royal Robe daylily

Hemerocallis × 'Stella de Oro', Stella de Oro daylily

Hosta × 'Blue Angel', Blue Angel hosta

Hyacinthus orientalis 'L'Innocence', L'Innocence white hyacinth

Iris pseudacorus, yellow flag iris

Iris sibirica, Siberian iris

Iris sibirica 'Butter and Sugar', Butter and Sugar Siberian iris

Miscanthus sacchariflorus, Japanese silver grass

Miscanthus sinensis 'Gracillimus', maiden grass

Miscanthus sinensis 'Strictus', porcupine grass

Narcissus pseudonarcissus, white daffodil

Rudbeckia fulgida var. *sullivantii* 'Goldsturm', Goldsturm black-eyed Susan

Rudbeckia hirta, black-eyed Susan

Sedum, stonecrop

Solidago rugosa 'Fireworks', Fireworks goldenrod

Stachys byzantina, lamb's ear

Symphyotrichum novae-angliae 'Purple Dome', Purple Dome aster

Symphyotrichum novi-belgii, New York aster

Tulipa 'White Dream', White Triumph tulip

Vinca minor, periwinkle

HERBS

Lavandula angustifolia, English lavender

Perovskia atriplicifolia 'Little Spire', Russian sage

Salvia leucophylla, purple sage

Salvia nemorosa 'East Friesland', East Friesland meadow sage

Salvia × sylvestris 'Mainacht', May Night salvia

GROUNDCOVER

Festuca glauca, blue fescue

Liriope muscari, lilyturf

Sustainability

LAND

Reclaimed brownfield as site for public park

Historical context reflected by marking original alignment of Lake Shore Drive with line of Bradford pear trees through the park's center

Centerpiece for commercial high-rise development in surrounding neighborhood

Erosion controlled by soil-stabilizing geotextiles and retaining walls that divert water

Healthy soils conserved, unhealthy soils amended

PLANTING

460 deciduous trees planted

Native plants used in ornamental gardens

Pesticide and fertilizer use minimized

Increased water and nutrient absorption by planting promoted through mycorrhizal fungi implemented in soil mix; carbohydrates for fungi provided, in turn, by planting

Plants allowed to go from seed to flower

Annual planting avoided

CARBON, ENERGY & AIR

Building energy use minimized and temperatures of urban areas reduced through planting

Regional material utilized, reducing emissions resulting from transportation

55,200 pounds of carbon—equal to emissions produced by 6.7 cars—sequestered annually by trees**

Pollutants controlled and retained during construction

WATER

76% of surfaces permeable

Up to 230,000 gallons of water—equivalent to the daily usage of 2,300 Americans—can be intercepted annually by trees*

Water usage reduced through low-water planting

WASTE

Sustainability in material manufacturing supported

Materials reused on-site when possible and unneeded materials recycled

Reusable vegetation, rocks, and soil diverted from disposal

ECONOMICS

Redevelopment effort that includes 4,950 residential units, 1,500 hotel rooms, 2.2 million square feet of gross commercial space, 770,000 square feet of retail space, and elementary school catalyzed

Maintenance savings achieved due to design strategy

Job and volunteer opportunities created on-site

SOCIAL

Alternative modes of transportation supported; cyclists and pedestrians traverse daily

Optimal site accessiblity, safety, and wayfinding provided through design

Visual amenity to tenants in surrounding towers

Average 4.5-star reviews on Yelp

Users and stakeholders engaged through community meetings prior to installation

Playa Vista

Playa Vista, California

Knit across two significant parcels of the two-thousand-acre former site of Howard Hughes's aircraft facility, Playa Vista is a series of interventions with distinct programs and uses: Playa Vista Central Park anchors a sixty-four-acre portion that also includes mixed-used developments the Campus at Playa Vista and the Collective, and across the larger site is situated the Randy Johnson Bluff Creek Fields. Together the open compositions denote the importance of gardens and public space within the urban fabric of Los Angeles.

Conceived as a public art installation, Playa Vista Central Park is organized into a sequence of discrete landscape experiences unified by a central spine and linear bands of specimen trees and organized around a function lawn and performance pavilion surrounded by bosques of shade trees. The nine-acre park includes, to the west of the lawn, sports courts, a playground, a soccer field, botanical gardens, water features, and a band shell. An immersive berm garden east of the green is composed of bold installations of Southern California plant material.

The Campus at Playa Vista, a significant 6.5-acre workplace parcel, is adjacent to and takes cues from the park, with verdant landscaped areas between structured parking and four buildings. These garden forecourts form a processional sequence for visitors walking from the ground level into the tenant lobbies. Richly detailed courtyards between the buildings utilize different combinations of paving materials and drought-tolerant plants to create a unique mood and identity for each entry. Second-floor terraces allow tenants to move freely from indoor to outdoor spaces, transforming the workplace, and fourth-floor terraces provide sweeping panoramas of the Santa Monica Mountains and downtown Los Angeles. Each parcel has direct access to or views toward Central Park, establishing a strong relationship between architecture and landscape.

A second commercial area, the Collective, is a two-parcel site with five buildings that stretch across its expanse. The site design is heavily bermed and draws inspiration from California coastal bluffs and foothills. The planting uses soft, lacy textures in silver and lush greens with highlights of purple and blue perennials. Mesquite trees along the main path evoke a canyon character. Courtyards contain a private interior zone within the promenade, protected by larger shade trees, to encourage outdoor collaboration. The materiality of the ground plane is expressed through pattern and texture, including rough stone edges that delineate the planting zone. The streetscape acts as a protective edge to the pavilions, with a palette of tipu trees and tall grasses, shrubs, and perennials.

Across the larger site, Randy Johnson Bluff Creek Fields, which borders the Bluff Creek Trail conservation area, utilizes a language of wood architectural features to visually connect it to the nature reserve. Rustic materials and plantings are deployed in this active recreational space, adding to the variety and texture of the ensemble of open spaces spanning Playa Vista.

Together, these open compositions, each with distinct programs and uses, denote the importance of gardens and public space within the urban fabric of Los Angeles.

Central Park

In Central Park, the berm gardens create an immersive landscape experience. A rhythm is established across the nine-acre composition that pairs sports-intensive activity areas with quieter spaces that encourage lingering, such as botanical gardens and water features.

Wide bands of specimen plantings are arranged in bold, vertical swaths that provide exuberant color and movement throughout the seasons.

The Campus at Playa Vista

Offering a welcome respite from Los Angeles's busy urban environment, this low-density district promotes connectivity to Central Park and the benefits of an indoor-outdoor office environment.

← 28 October | 11:49 a.m.

→ 17 December | 4:53 p.m.

← Plantings add a three-dimensional, sculptural quality to the terraces, which offer sweeping panoramas from the Santa Monica Mountains to downtown Los Angeles. → Richly detailed courtyards contain distinct combinations of drought-tolerant plantings to imbue a unique mood and identity throughout each site.

The Collective

A tonal palette of native California species
is paired with rough-edged stone flooring and
paving to evoke the nearby canyons and coastal
bluffs within the five-building ensemble.

Shaded walkways and layered plantings create color, shadow, and fragrance along the visitor path, encouraging collaboration outdoors.

Randy Johnson Bluff Creek Fields

Reflecting its proximity to an adjacent
trail system and conservation area, Randy
Johnson Bluff Creek Fields uses a rustic and
naturalistic planting and furnishings palette.

← 29 April | 3:56 p.m.

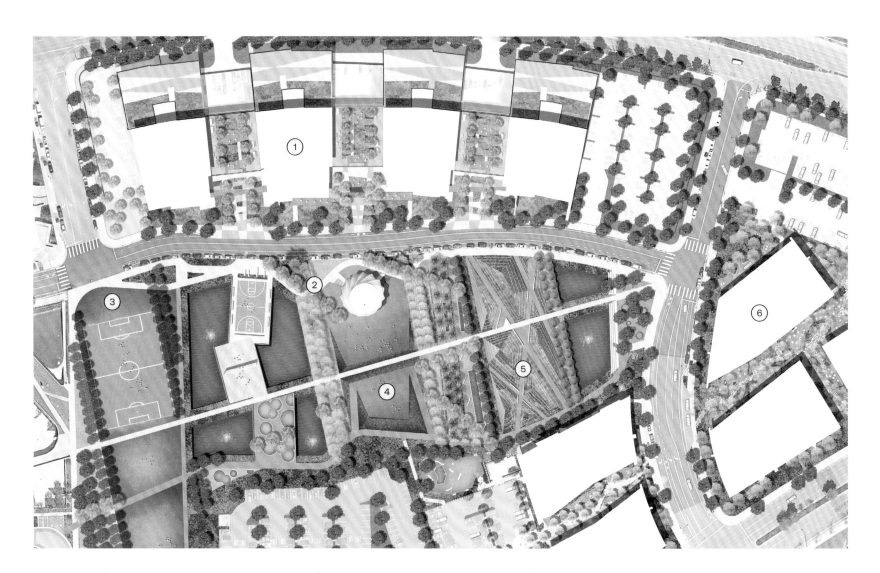

1. The Campus at Playa Vista
2. Central Park
3. Sport fields

4. Event lawn
5. Berm garden
6. The Collective

Not shown:
Randy Johnson Bluff Creek Fields

Plantings

TREES

Jacaranda, jacaranda

Pinus canariensis, Canary Island pine

Platanus × acerifolia, London plane tree

Platanus racemosa, California sycamore

Quercus suber, cork oak

Tabebuia impetiginosa, pink trumpet tree

SHRUBS, GRASSES & GROUNDCOVERS

Agave attenuata, foxtail agave

Canna × generalis 'Lucifer', Lucifer dwarf canna

Festuca californica, California fescue

Festuca glauca, blue fescue

Heuchera 'Caramel', Caramel coral bells

Heuchera 'Green Spice', Green Spice coral bells

Heuchera 'Peach Flambe', Peach Flambe coral bells

Heuchera 'Moonlight', Moonlight coral bells

× *Heucherella* 'Alabama Sunrise' (PPAF), Alabama Sunrise coral bells

Iris douglasiana, Douglas iris

Juncus filiformis 'Spiralis', corkscrew rush

Leymus condensatus 'Canyon Prince', Canyon Prince wild rye

Miscanthus transmorrisonensis, evergreen eulalia

Muhlenbergia rigens, deer grass

Phormium tenax 'Jack Spratt', Jack Spratt New Zealand flax

Scirpus cernuus, fiber optic grass

Senecio mandraliscae, blue chalksticks

Vinca minor 'Alba', dwarf periwinkle

Buchloe dactyloides 'UC Verde', buffalo grass

AQUATIC PLANTS

Canna × generalis 'Lucifer', Lucifer dwarf canna

Carex comans 'Green', New Zealand sedge

Eleocharis montevidensis, sand spikerush

Iris ensata 'Blue' (Aquatic), blue Japanese iris

Juncus effusus 'Unicorn', Unicorn soft rush

Marsilea minuta, dwarf waterclover

Nymphaea odorata, American white water lily

Schoenoplectus subterminalis, swaying bulrush

LAWN

Cynodon dactylon 'Santa Ana', hybrid Bermuda grass

Muscari armeniacum, grape hyacinth

Stenotaphrum secundatum, St. Augustine grass

Sustainability

LAND

Erosion controlled by soil-stabilizing geotextiles, plants for root stability, and retaining walls that divert water

Healthy soils conserved and unhealthy soils amended through remediation, testing, and extraction of methane, resulting in substantial savings

WATER

Stormwater runoff pollutants captured by vegetated bioswales in parking lot

Water usage reduced through low-water planting

PLANTING

Seeds sourced locally

435 trees planted

Fertilizer and pesticide use minimized

Increased water and nutrient absorption by planting promoted through mycorrhizal fungi implemented in soil mix; carbohydrates for fungi provided, in turn, by planting

Plants allowed to go from seed to flower

Annual planting avoided

CARBON, ENERGY & AIR

Building energy use minimized by planting

Regional material utilized, reducing emissions resulting from transportation

Concrete and plant material recycled

Light pollution reduced by use of full cutoff fixtures

52,000 pounds of carbon sequestered annually by trees**

WASTE

Waste reduced by supporting sustainable manufacturing, salvaging material used on-site, reusing material, and recycling end-of-project waste

SOCIAL

Optimal site accessibility, safety, and wayfinding achieved through design

Regional trails and social areas easily accessible for pedestrian connections between spaces

Capturing the Spirit of Place

Sunnylands Center
and Gardens

Rancho Mirage, California

On a nine-acre parcel, a botanical garden with fifty-three thousand specimens and walking trails creates a place for relaxation and discovery.

The harsh desert climate typically evokes the dull colors of scrubland. By contrast, the two-hundred-acre estate of the late philanthropist Walter Annenberg and his wife, Leonore, existed as a highly maintained collection of green spaces tied to its midcentury residence and guesthouses. A fifteen-acre parcel adjacent to the estate was an opportunity to challenge this ecology and create a place of relaxation and discovery in a contemporary aesthetic. Working closely with Mrs. Annenberg, the intent was to welcome visitors to the grounds at a new exhibition pavilion and invite reflection in the surrounding garden spaces. Today the gardens at Sunnylands surprise visitors with their variety and vibrant hues, while displaying native species in bold strokes.

The quiet expression of the pavilion, designed by Frederick Fisher and Partners, contrasts with the vivid botanical garden, which features fifty-three thousand handpicked specimens from over seventy species of native and arid-adapted plants. Organic and free-flowing at the edges of the site, the lines of hardscape surfaces and planting beds take on a geometric precision as they approach the building. An adjacent event terrace and lawn offer views of the San Jacinto Mountains. Flanking the terrace, twin reflecting basins mirror the expansive desert sky, lower the ambient temperature, and fill the area with the relaxing sound of running water. More than 1.25 miles of walking trails lead visitors past the event lawn, beneath flowering palo verde desert trees, to a labyrinth garden, a performance circle, and interpretive displays of native plants.

The desert location is an essential component of the sustainability framework, which features restored habitat, a high-efficiency capillary irrigation system, soil moisture monitoring, stormwater retention, geothermal wells, a significant photovoltaic array, and an on-site green waste recycling program. Sunnylands Center and Gardens is a pilot project for the Sustainable SITES Initiative, is LEED Gold certified, and uses only approximately 20 percent of its water allocation from the Coachella Valley Water District.

→ The entire composition of the
garden unfolds just beyond the
Annenberg Estate, with the San
Jacinto Mountains in the distance.

↑ 21 April | 11:36 a.m.

In mid-spring, the blooming groves of palo
verde trees ring the main lawn in a profusion
of yellow, offering visitors a glorious sight as
they explore the gardens.

← 19 March | 6:24 p.m.
→ 4 May | 5:54 p.m.

Nestled in a grove of hybrid mesquite, the labyrinth is a place of quiet reflection.

← 1 May | 12:16 p.m.

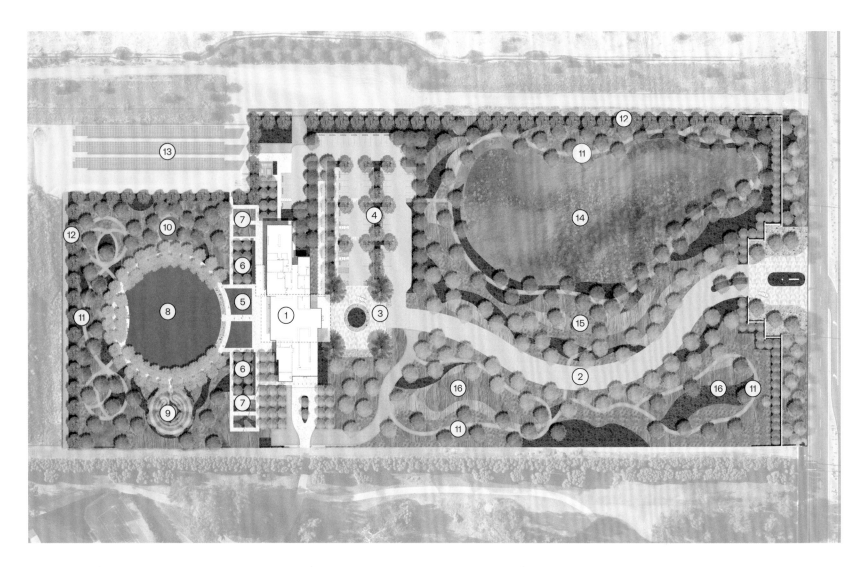

1. Visitor center
2. Entry drive
3. Entry court
4. Parking
5. Terrace
6. Reflecting basins

7. Specimen gardens
8. Great lawn
9. Labyrinth
10. Performance circle
11. Botanic walk
12. Texas ebony hedge

13. Solar field
14. Wildflower meadow
15. Berm garden
16. Stormwater retention basin

Plantings

TREES

Acacia farnesiana, sweet acacia

Parkinsonia 'Desert Museum', thornless hybrid palo verde

Parkinsonia praecox, hybrid palo brea

Pithecellobium flexicaule, Texas ebony

Prosopis hybrid, hybrid mesquite

ORNAMENTAL PLANTING

Agave americana, century plant

Agave deserti, desert agave

Agave desmettiana, smooth agave

Agave geminiflora, twin-flowered agave

Agave macroacantha, black-spined agave

Agave neomexicana, New Mexico century plant

Agave parryi, Parry's agave

Agave parryi var. *truncata*, artichoke agave

Agave titanota, chalk agave

Agave salmiana, giant agave

Agave 'Sharkskin', sharkskin agave

Aloe hybrid, blue elf aloe

Aloe striata, coral aloe

Aloe vera, medicinal aloe

Asclepias subulata, desert milkweed

Bulbine frutescens, orange bulbine

Cleistocactus silvestri, silver torch

Dalea greggii, trailing smokebush

Dasylirion quadrangulatum, Mexican grass tree

Echinocactus grusonii, golden barrel

Echinopsis pachanoi, San Pedro cactus

Euphorbia antisyphilitica, candelilla

Euphorbia rigida, gopher plant

Euphorbia resinifera, Moroccan mound

Fouquieria splendens, ocotillo

Hesperaloe funifera, giant hesperaloe

Hesperaloe parviflora, red hesperaloe

Leucophyllum frutescens, green cloud

Leucophyllum hybrid, heavenly cloud

Leucophyllum langmaniae 'Lynn's Legacy', Texas ranger

Leucophyllum langmaniae 'Rio Bravo', Rio Bravo ranger

Leucophyllum laevigatum, Chihuahuan sage

Leucophyllum pruinosum, Sierra bouquet

Larrea tridentata, creosote bush

Nolina texana, bear grass

Nolina nelsonii, blue bear grass

Opuntia microdasys, bunny ears prickly pear

Pedilanthus macrocarpus, lady slipper

Santolina viridis, green santolina

Tetraneuris acaulis/scaposa, angelita daisy

Yucca rostrata, beaked yucca

Yucca whipplei, Our Lord's candle

Yucca pallida, pale-leaf yucca

SPECIALTY CACTUS

Agave celsii 'Multicolor', multicolor agave

Aloe ferox, bitter aloe

Espostoa melanostele, wooly torch

Euphorbia caput-medusae, Medusa's head

Ferocactus glaucescens, blue barrel

Ferocactus pringlei stainesii, red barrel

Lophocereus schottii, whisker cactus

Lophocereus schottii monstrose, totem pole

Mammillaria pringlei, golden pincushion

Notocactus leninghausii, golden ball

Pachycereus pringlei, giant cardon

Stenocereus marginatus, Mexican fence post

Stenocereus thurberi, organ pipe

DESERT SEED MIX

Abronia villosa, sand verbena

Achnatherum hymenoides, Indian ricegrass

Aristida purpurea, purple three-awn

Atriplex polycarpa, saltbush

Baileya multiradiata, desert marigold

Bouteloua gracilis, blue grama

Encelia farinosa, brittlebush

Eschscholzia californica, California poppy

Larrea tridentata, creosote bush

Lasthenia californica, California goldfields

Oenothera deltoides, desert primrose

Salvia columbariae, chia

Sustainability

LAND

Ecological conditions of degraded site restored

Habitat created for threatened and endangered species, including cottontail rabbits, jackrabbits, desert iguanas, monarch butterflies, hawks, and vermilion flycatchers

Erosion controlled by soil-stabilizing geotextiles to promote root stability

Soil management plan establishing protected zones, conserved soil, and amended soil informed by predesign site assessment

WATER

20% of water allocation from Coachella Valley Water District utilized

100% on-site stormwater retention

Water use reduced through high-efficiency capillary irrigation zones independently controlled by soil moisture sensors

Water capture seamlessly integrated into garden pathways and planting design

Water usage reduced through low-water planting

PLANTING

53,000 arid-landscape plants planted, including 70 different plant and tree species

617 trees planted

Seeds locally sourced and adapted to climate

Fertilizer and pesticide use minimized

Annual planting avoided

Plants allowed to go from seed to flower

Increased water and nutrient absorption by planting promoted through mycorrhizal fungi implemented in soil mix; carbohydrates for fungi provided, in turn, by planting

CARBON, ENERGY & AIR

Heating and cooling of the center by closed-loop temperature transfer through geothermic system with 96 wells 396 feet below the event lawn

Solar energy captured in photovoltaic fields

72,000 pounds of carbon—equal to emissions from 8.9 cars per year—sequestered annually by trees**

Regional material utilized, reducing emissions resulting from transportation

Energy usage of the center minimized by planting vegetation around the building

WASTE

Waste reduced by supporting sustainable manufacturing, salvaging material used on-site, reusing material, and recycling end-of-project waste

SOCIAL

9 acres of desert gardens created

Major events, educational and family programs, garden walks, yoga classes, a speaker series, and art exhibitions hosted at the center

Alternative modes of transportation supported by providing buses during events, preferred parking for ride-sharing, and electric vehicle parking

Optimal site accessibility, safety, and wayfinding achieved through design

Hall Winery
St. Helena, California

This historic vineyard in the heart of Napa Valley has been transformed from an industrial winemaking site into a lively and inviting destination whose campus of new and renovated buildings and garden rooms punctuated by outdoor sculpture sensitively blends the contemporary and the historical. Outdated prefab metal buildings and run-down structures have been replaced by an airy, glass-walled visitor center, and a nineteenth-century stone building from the original winery is given fresh purpose. This updated composition of architecture, art, and landscape immerses the visitor in the terroir, dissolving the boundary between the organic vineyards and outdoor gathering areas.

Low, crisp limestone walls and bermed planting draw visitors from Highway 29 to the interior of the site, where a sinuous lane planted with grasses leads into the parking area and around an island anchored by a preserved valley oak surrounded by grasses and lavender. Rounding this island gives visitors a glimpse of the entire composition of historic and new buildings, together with long vistas to the garden areas. The curving entrance road also separates cars from the buildings and gardens to encourage relaxation and exploration of the entire grounds before and after the tastings.

The landscape parti marries structured outdoor spaces with meandering pathways and dynamic movement. The 150-year-old, thirty-five-acre vineyard is restored and reorganized around the new visitor center and a five-acre landscape composition of outdoor rooms off a 6,500-square-foot great lawn. This gathering lawn balances the alternating impressions of openness and enclosure that flow throughout the site and acts as a flexible canvas for a wide variety of musical, culinary, and cultural events.

Twin rows of red oak trees surround the historic stone Bergfeld building, which sits adjacent to the great lawn, and create a sight line west across the lawn to *Reflection of Life*, a long granite reflection fountain created by artist Jesús Moroles. Beneath the trees, a silvery palette of hardy grasses and high mountain perennials adds dimension.

Strolling farther into the site, visitors arrive at a sensory garden, which sets the tone for immersion in landscape and art. In the garden, small-scale plantings and textured grasses are woven together around sculptures by Molly Chappellet. A frame of existing and newly planted sycamore trees defines the edge of the garden and turns the focus on the art.

Along the northern edge of the site, limestone walls delineate three outdoor courts: a cutting garden, a grove of olive trees, and a kitchen garden that supplies the campus's kitchens with vegetables and herbs. To the west, on a curving gravel terrace—dubbed the "oceanfront" terrace—along the edge of the vineyard, visitors are offered umbrellas and lounge chairs to relax next to Moroles's serene fountain and view the production vineyards more closely. From this vantage, the Mayacamas Mountains are carefully framed.

On a historic vineyard in the heart of Napa Valley, an updated landscape immerses the visitor in the terroir.

← 15 April | 6:12 p.m.

← The entry drive brings cars from Highway 29 along a newly conceived planted lane, with stunning views of the Mayacamas Mountains and the vineyards. → As visitors move into the site, art and landscape come together to enhance the sensory experience of the wine.

← Wide pathways from the parking area to the tasting rooms encourage guests to experience the landscape before and after tasting the acclaimed wines. → A silvery palette of hardy grasses, small-leafed trees, and perennials creates a multidimensional passage across the site.

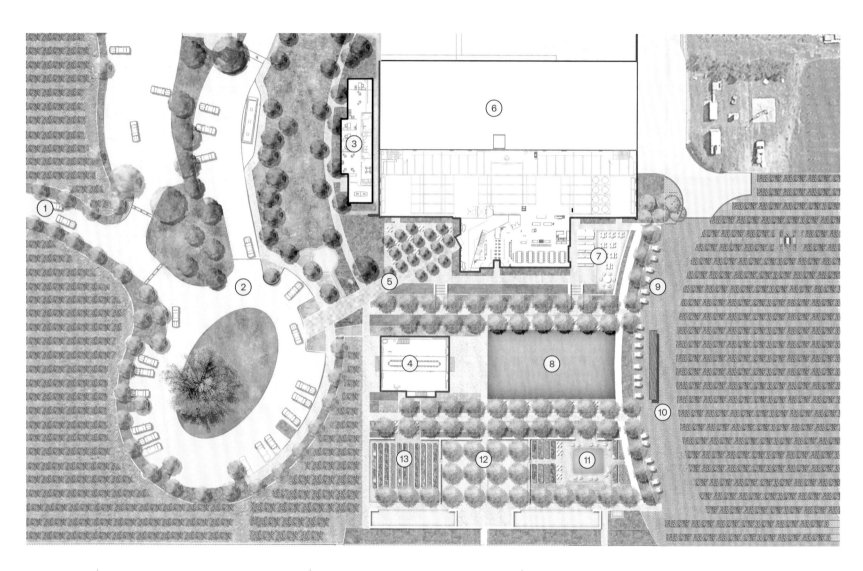

1. Site entry
2. Auto court
3. Offices
4. Bergfeld building
5. Entry grove

6. Visitor/tasting center
7. Dining court
8. Event lawn
9. "Oceanfront" terrace
10. *Reflection of Life*

11. Cutting garden
12. Olive grove
13. Vegetable garden

Plantings

SHRUBS

Echium fastuosum, pride of Madeira

Forestiera neomexicana, New Mexican privet

Leucophyllum langmaniae 'Lynn's Legacy',
Texas ranger

Trichostema lanatum, woolly blue curls

Westringia fruticosa 'Wynyabbie Gem',
coast rosemary

PERENNIALS

Buddleja davidii 'Purple Prince', butterfly bush

Coreopsis grandiflora 'Double Sunburst',
large-flowered tickseed

Lavandula angustifolia 'Lavender Lady', English
lavender

Lavandula dentata, French lavender

Lavandula 'Goodwin Creek Gray', lavender

Lavandula stoechas, Spanish lavender

Liatris spicata, marsh blazing star

Nepeta × *faassenii*, catmint

Perovskia atriplicifolia, azure sage

Rudbeckia hirta, gloriosa daisy

Salvia leucantha, Mexican bush sage

Salvia nemorosa 'Blue Hill', garden sage

Salvia nemorosa, 'Ostfriesland',
East Friesland sage

GRASSES

Leymus condensatus 'Canyon Prince', wild rye

Miscanthus sinensis 'Morning Light', silver grass

Nassella tenuissima, Mexican feather grass

Pennisetum orientale, oriental fountain grass

CUTTING GARDEN

Agastache foeniculum, anise hyssop

Osteospermum, African daisy

Coreopsis verticillate 'Moonbeam', coreopsis

Echinacea purpurea, purple coneflower

Gardenia jasminoides 'Frostproof', gardenia

Kniphofia caulescens, red hot poker

Lantana camara 'Dwarf Yellow', lantana

Lithodora diffusa 'Grace Ward', lithodora

Miscanthus sinensis 'Adagio', Adagio silver grass

Monarda didyma, scarlet bee balm

Nepeta racemosa 'Blue Wonder', catmint

Penstemon campanulatus, beardtongue

Rosa × 'Betty White', hybrid tea rose Betty White

Rosa × 'Radwhite', White Knock Out rose

Salvia greggii, autumn sage

Verbena 'Tapien Pure White', verbena

VEGETABLES

Allium cepa, red torpedo onion

Allium sativum, garlic

Asparagus officinalis, asparagus

Beta vulgaris var. *cicla*, Swiss chard

Brassica oleracea italica × *alboglabra*, broccolini

Brassica oleracea botrytis, Cheddar cauliflower

Brassica oleracea gemmifera, brussels sprouts

Brassica oleracea italica, romanesco broccoli

Brassica oleracea var. *gongylodes*, kohlrabi

Brassica juncea, mustard greens

Daucus carota subsp. *sativus*, carrot

Lactuca sativa var. *capitata*, Buttercrunch lettuce

Lactuca sativa var. *crispa*, Red Sails lettuce

Lactuca sativa var. *longifolia*, romaine lettuce

Lactuca sativa 'Oak Leaf', green oak leaf lettuce

Lactuca sativa var. *longifolia*, red romaine lettuce

Pisum sativum var. *saccharatum*, snow pea

GROUNDCOVER

Arctostaphylos densiflora 'Emerald Carpet',
carpet manzanita

Sustainability

LAND

Existing historic nineteenth-century buildings integrated with new high-performance hospitality and winemaking facility

Soils amended and protection zones maintained

WATER

All processed water routed to settling point, then aerated and filtered for landscape irrigation

Stormwater mitigated by site design

48% of surfaces permeable

Water usage reduced through low-water planting

PLANTING

3 legacy trees at entry preserved

185 trees planted

Increased water and nutrient absorption by planting promoted through mycorrhizal fungi implemented in soil mix; carbohydrates for fungi provided, in turn, by planting

Fertilizer and pesticide use minimized

Annual planting avoided

Plants allowed to go from seed to flower

Cut flowers, vegetables, olives, fruits, and herbs produced by organic garden

CARBON, ENERGY & AIR

22,200 pounds of carbon—equivalent to emissions produced by driving 30,199 miles in a passenger vehicle—sequestered annually by trees**

SOCIAL

Optimal site accessibility, safety, and wayfinding achieved through design

Increase in visitors and activities due to new outdoor program spaces

Visitors are drawn to the world-class collection of sculpture on the site

Seeing the Unseen:
In Conversation with OJB

Bradford McKee

*Bradford McKee is a design
journalist and former editor of*
Landscape Architecture Magazine

My first up-close look at the landscape architecture of OJB was at Sunnylands. Long the home of Walter and Leonore Annenberg, Sunnylands was an unusual, nearly mythical place, called a western Camp David for its guest list of presidents, royalty, and movie stars who arrived over the years. It is now a foundation with its headquarters on those grounds. I visited in March, and it was warm and bright. As I drove into the visitor center compound, I was engulfed by floods of desert grasses and explosions of wildflowers along flowing slopes carpeted with succulent plants. The thin trunks of palo verde trees twisted up from the tough ground into feathery canopies. This riot of xeric life receded before the visitor center itself, a flat, rational arrangement of paths, lawns, and pools around a gleaming white pavilion.

At Sunnylands, you see the work of a landscape architecture firm that is in clear control of its palette and of itself. The firm, now with five offices, is like this landscape in that there are many dynamic supporting parts that generally go unseen. James Burnett founded the firm in 1989 and has built it on several straightforward principles that have sustained its growth: restorative spaces, shared leadership, operating below means, and, most important, design first. The firm and the signature projects shown in these pages are well-known among professional peers and clients seeking prestige, but the firm has tended to keep its head down, working on a broader array of project types and ever in pursuit, in Burnett's words to his team, of adventure.

The times are less low-key for OJB now as it enters its thirty-second year of operation. In 2015, the American Society of Landscape Architects honored OJB with the Firm Award, and in 2016 conferred its Design Medal, an individual honor, on James Burnett. Most recently, OJB was named the recipient of its most high-profile honor yet, the 2020 National Design Award for Landscape Architecture presented by the Cooper Hewitt, Smithsonian Design Museum, which recognizes designers annually across disciplines. The excitement surrounding the National Design Award, in particular, and the imminent publication of this monograph were very much in the air when I joined OJB's partners in late summer of 2020 to talk about the firm's history and its growth between the modest health care gardens of its origins and the feats of urban transformation for which is it respected today.

ORIGINS AND GROWTH

BRADFORD MCKEE: We're together here just after the firm's thirtieth anniversary. To cap off that milestone, you've just been awarded the 2020 National Design Award for Landscape Architecture by the Cooper Hewitt, so major congratulations are in order.

Let's talk about the firm's beginnings.

JAMES BURNETT: Thanks, Brad. Thirty years have gone by in a blink of an eye, but the things that drove me to go out on my own are the same things that drive the firm today. I was five years into my career as a landscape architect, working for a large multidisciplinary firm in Houston, Caudill Rowlett Scott [CRS]. I had the good fortune to be introduced to Peter Walker, who was leading design on several projects we were supporting. It struck me how Pete led with a design-first philosophy, and I truly admired this passion. Over the course of working together, I told him I was going to pursue a graduate degree in architecture. Pete challenged me to rethink my decision, telling me, "We need you in landscape." After meeting with Dan Kiley and others who were leading the field at the time, I decided to recommit to the idea that landscape could have just as big an impact as architecture and made the decision to go out on my own. The first six months were eye-opening because I discovered that landing great projects doesn't happen right away in a solo practice.

My first break came because I rented a space in the office of the architecture firm Watkins Carter Hamilton in Houston, and Kirk Hamilton asked me to be part of a pursuit for a new 160-bed replacement hospital in Texarkana. During the interview I had a big role in presenting ideas about the creation of a campus that focused on health and wellness through healing, restorative gardens. We won the commission, and that project launched our practice with a specialty in health care design.

Around the same time, I watched my mother suffer while battling cancer and ultimately die in a poorly designed hospital environment. This hospital had no space for staff, visitors, or patients to get outdoors, connect with nature, and breathe fresh air. The hospital entries were crowded with smokers, and the site was covered with parking lots, garages, and buildings. At that time, few designers were looking at the humanistic experience in health care. One notable exception was Edward Durell Stone, whose remarkable Community Hospital in Monterey, California, has interior atriums filled with natural light and water. But there were only a handful of landscape architects designing for health care. So that's how the practice got its start.

MCKEE: You mention the term "design-first." Talk about that notion a little as an aspiration and what it means.

BURNETT: From the beginning, I have embraced the idea that solving the challenges of the project through a thoughtful design process was the most important goal. Of course, we have to begin with a deep analysis of all the forces surrounding the site and problem—the climate, the ecology, and the program. And we have to make certain that the spaces perform at a high level. But we are always striving to go beyond function and capture the spirit of the place. We want to create moments of unexpected discovery. It might be the sound of water, or the smell of a tree in bloom, or the shade that its canopy provides. We want to encourage people to linger, to spend time alone and together. We always aspire to imbue an idea with our passion and energy, and then support and champion it.

In 2001, when I first walked the site of the Salk Institute in La Jolla, California, with Louis Kahn's partners David Rinehart and Jack MacAllister to talk about a new master plan, I was struck by their conviction to remain true to Kahn's vision for the site. The public experience of the grounds is intimately tied to the private moments of reflection and connection. The ground, the sky, and the quiet rule of water are magically composed. They capture the light and spirit of the place like no other. Finding that magic, to me, is design-first. And we have built the practice together with like-minded collaborators who value the same way of thinking. We strive in all our commissions to give the client something that they never imagined they could have beyond meeting the brief. At the same time, finding those moments of transformation that surprise those who experience our gardens is one of our greatest joys.

MCKEE: Tell me a bit about how your collaborative practice came to be. What were some of the ideas that brought you together and how have they changed since the early days?

CHIP TRAGESER: I think the biggest driver for collaboration is our love of dialogue around the design challenge. I joined Jim in 1990 and was instantly drawn to the kind of big thinking that characterized the projects. We were lucky to have some pivotal opportunities very early in the game. One of the first significant projects I worked on was the master plan for London's Canary Wharf with Phil Enquist at SOM Chicago. Working with their planning team in London led to an opportunity for a master plan for Lakeshore East, a prominent twenty-eight-acre site in downtown Chicago. At the heart of the project, we designed a six-acre park that became a shared open space for the expansive development. It set the stage for us to examine how large-scale parks could impact cities, which has continued to be an important line of inquiry for us.

KYLE FIDDELKE: Similarly, my early opportunities in the firm shaped our development in a big way. I joined the firm in 1992, and one of my first projects was a downtown office block in Houston. At first blush, it was a pretty straightforward assignment, but we studied the streetscape and how we could improve the public realm. This central tenet hasn't changed: we are still interested in how people experience open space and how to make our cities, our workplaces, and our shared public spaces better.

JERECK BOSS: Before I joined the firm in 2004, I had worked in a more traditional multidisciplinary firm, but I was looking for someone who was examining landscape and collaboration through a different lens. I had seen Jim in Spacemaker Press books and *Landscape Architecture Magazine* and was intrigued by the new ideas about health and wellness that were coming out of the firm. More importantly, Jim told me early on that there's always power in the pen, so never to be afraid to draw. This has held true for all of us as the firm has grown and changed. We have equal ideas and we welcome all voices in the design dialogue.

CODY KLEIN: Oh, I got that talk, too, and it always stuck with me! The best idea should always win. It doesn't matter where the idea germinates. There are threads of creativity that can come from anywhere. It is important to tap into the collective knowledge and creativity and experience of the team.

DILLON DIERS: The first project I worked on was Sunnylands, and the first meeting I ever went to was with Mrs. Annenberg. But Jim opened up the dialogue and made sure that every voice was heard, including mine. Now I am especially attuned to providing the same opportunity for our younger professionals. It's how we keep the openness to new ideas at the forefront and continue to challenge each other.

MEG LEVY: From an operations point of view, we balance this design creativity with down-to-earth management.

We operate below our means, for example. It helps keep us grounded and, in fact, allows us the freedom to explore.

BURNETT: I want to add one more thing. There is a spirit of adventure in everything we do. We keep trying new things, not for their novelty, but to keep advancing our knowledge and our craft. We want to choose projects with people who are interested in the same kind of innovations.

Dan Kiley gave me some of the greatest advice for practice: "Never work for the money first. It'll kill you. You'll end up compromising everything you do." We have built our firm on this premise. We try to remember that it is an adventure like no other.

KLEIN: It has certainly been an adventure. I came to OJB in 2011, after having met Jim when I was working at a local landscape architecture firm in Oklahoma City, providing assistance on the ground for a series of increasingly complex projects that have changed the city in truly unexpected ways. These include a new headquarters for Devon Energy Corporation; the revitalization of the city's most important park, Myriad Botanical Gardens; and a complete redesign of the city's downtown streetscape—all 180 acres of it.

The projects work in synergy, from the edges of the street to the green spaces of all sizes of gardens. It has transformed the downtown into a walkable and accessible place, where shaded sidewalks and shared green space are the new public face of Oklahoma City. People connect to these moments in their city with great pride, and the result is that businesses are returning downtown, along with an influx of new residents.

MCKEE: Tell me more about the idea of public benefit that drives so much of your work. How do you decide whether a project will allow you to provide it?

BURNETT: We know that being in nature changes us, though not all of the reasons why. And we are committed to the premise that access to green space is a human right. Especially in our urban centers, having access to a park or green space can connect people to the natural world and to each other. Our work in the public arena has expanded with our commitment to creating more of these kinds of spaces. It is the most satisfying work we do—creating great public open space. We don't view public benefit as an afterthought. Even in private work spaces, owners have seen the benefits of blurring the boundary between building and garden. Studies have shown that views of green space can change your physiology in a dramatic way and shift your brain into a different mode of processing. The benefits accrue for everyone.

We are in an emerging field of practice, and we are just starting to understand the incredible benefits that nature creates for us.

TRAGESER: We believe in creating spaces for people. We want to think beyond the idea of a garden for a select few. Even the street is a shared realm. It should be beautiful, and it should work for everyone.

DIERS: And the benefits continue to accrue after the opening day excitement and energy. The spaces must sustain themselves over time and be loved by the community. You know it's been successful and has matured when the community fully adopts it and embraces it in their own way. That's a spiritual connection between people and landscape.

MCKEE: Earlier, Jim, you had mentioned these dreadful medical care environments and the ability of a small garden in a medical setting to change someone's day for the better. Can you tell me more about bringing change on a larger scale, like public spaces in cities such as Dallas, where

Arjay Miller Arboretum, Ford Motor Company, Dearborn, Michigan

Klyde Warren Park replaced a huge section of highway in the middle of the city? How is that thinking different?

BURNETT: Now, as ever, I think changing a city is a noble and necessary idea. Cities need larger open spaces for people to recharge. In Dallas, that highway site was the big divide that separated the downtown Arts District from Uptown.

Aside from the technical challenge of building a park on top of a section of highway, we talked a lot about the specifics of how people might use the space, who would go there, and how they would get there. We had to look at all the interrelated networks and systems that make up the city center. There were many questions about whether this park would be successful. Because neighborhoods were bisected by highway spaces, it was difficult for people to imagine how the gash in the city fabric could be healed. But the park has become the new heart of downtown because it filled that need for people to have a place of their own. Neighborhoods are reconnected, and cultural buildings that turned their back to the highway now have a vibrant park at their front door.

MCKEE: Klyde Warren is one of those projects that changes how people look at city infrastructure. It's a total demonstration of the art of the possible.

BURNETT: It's good to talk about how cities work for people. We were able to take the unseen and make it seen. Repairing the city was about connecting people across this gulch and rethinking the spaces that had been ceded to cars. People were not crossing those bridges on foot. Everyone was in a car.

TRAGESER: It's basically made that area of Dallas walkable for the first time in decades. Walkability in city centers is very important. The past few years have seen the call

for greater access to public parks, including the Trust for Public Land's initiative campaigning for access to a park within a ten-minute walk of every home. The Paris model has gone even further, with a vision for the fifteen-minute city. This advocates for car-free transit and pedestrian infrastructure for all city residents. The model holds potential to build the city's economy and strengthen the communities, recreation, and health of all of its citizens.

MCKEE: I want to talk about the firm's culture. It's quite intentional. To start with one interesting detail, I hear your offices change the studio seating every so often.

LEVY: When I started, we were a small group of twelve people in one space. Now we have over ninety people spread across five offices. We stay connected by keeping the lines of communication open. That is due in large part to Jim's leadership from the beginning of the practice. To keep this working, mentoring is hugely important. It allows people to develop their points of view. People who are fresh out of school have equal opportunity to have their perspective heard and appreciated. This group of leaders is fostering the next generation of leaders. Even though we've grown in size and complexity, we have also grown to become better mentors. That's necessary so we can leave a lasting imprint beyond our time, right?

We do shake up the teams quite a bit. If someone has a desire to work on a different typology or for a different leader, they are encouraged to do that.

CLAUDIA THOMÉ: In Houston, we move around quite a bit more because our space is much larger. I think shuffling our team helps keep them engaged. It gives them an opportunity to be a part of different teams. It helps with collaboration and exposing the team to new processes and new ways of thinking.

Pathline Park, Sunnyvale, California

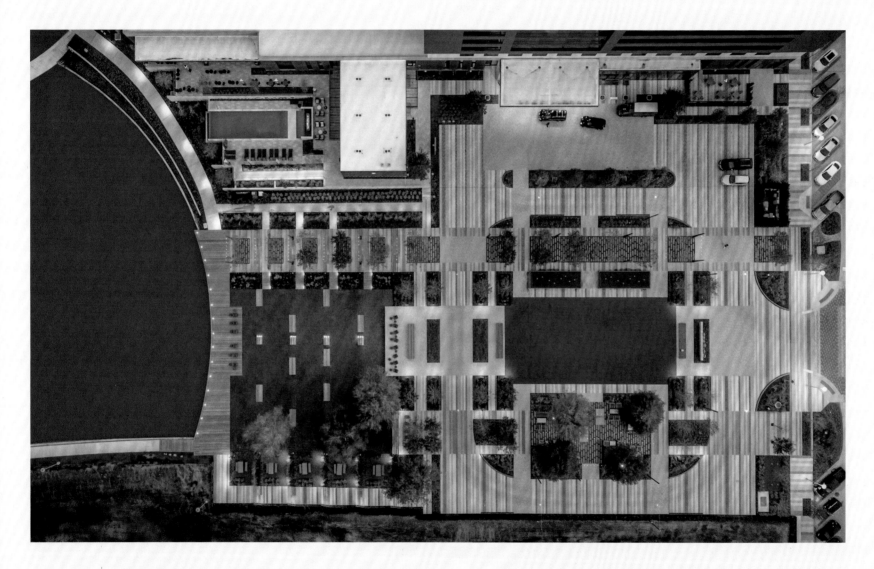

City Place at Springwoods Village
Spring, Texas

MCKEE: How does intelligence from the entire firm feed into specific projects? What is the culture with respect to open commentary or review on a given project? I've picked up that it occurs. Is it scheduled or does it happen spontaneously? Does it happen among the various offices?

BURNETT: People grow and learn faster when they feed off each other. In the past ten years, we've started each commission with more analysis and research. It's very exciting to keep digging down into the layers of a project. And there's more to it than landscape now. We're expected to know about fundraising and real estate values and understand the politics of a community along with the traditional analysis. It is a different game now. When we go into a meeting, we talk about not only the design, but also all of the forces that play a role in shaping the solution. The success of our work extends beyond the built environment.

MCKEE: What are some of the disciplines that are needed?

BOSS: Every day, we learn more about how to sustain and maintain landscapes, from soil specifications to continuing care to activation planning. Our team now includes specialists from across the technical spectrum, from materials science to community engagement.

MCKEE: Let's talk about continuing care and why maintenance is an increasingly necessary service in the scope of work. These spaces have perishable material in them, right? Everything's changing all the time.

TRAGESER: Landscape is constantly changing and evolving. Having somebody who stays close with the client and the contractor to maintain our projects is key. Our continuing care advisor is a horticulturist, and that has helped us and our clients to maintain gardens at a high level. As you note, plants need care throughout their lifetime to thrive

and flourish. We want to make sure that our gardens can continue to change and grow over time. They are living and breathing entities that need this care.

DIERS: Everything we learn builds upon itself. We dig into the performance of our landscapes and evaluate them post-occupancy with a wide range of criteria. Every project advances our knowledge and helps us improve our next project.

MCKEE: Let's hear about OJB Lab and how it originated in 2015.

BURNETT: The seeds of OJB Lab grew out of a desire to analyze our work more fully and move beyond the established sustainability certification systems. We developed a list of metrics to evaluate infrastructure, environmental, social, and cultural factors. We continue to analyze every project through these metrics and build on our knowledge and performance in successive projects.

MCKEE: So much of that research and just plain project investigation goes unseen by the public, despite the high visibility of your landscapes. What kinds of things do people not see that you wish they did?

FIDDELKE: The coordination and collaboration with other disciplines and specialty consultants consume a considerable amount of our time. There are utilities, below-grade structures, architectural and building components, soil sciences, horticulture, lighting, and economics that all influence the work we do and the final product we produce.

Being in nature changes us. . . . And we are committed to the premise that access to green space is a human right.

KLEIN: All of our projects have real budgets and constraints. Some of the most complex elements of a project are not the most obvious. I've often thought that most people who enjoy our work might never recognize why. It is the intangibles that are sometimes the most compelling for users—and are some of the most difficult aspects to achieve.

MCKEE: How do those research frontiers figure into what's ahead for OJB?

LEVY: We have evolved as not only a practice but also an industry. We are in a position where we can influence, where we can transform how landscape architecture is viewed. We're not just about traditional landscape design. We must be the influencers and agents of change, looking outside of our profession for inspiration.

BURNETT: Equity and access are critical to the future of the profession and to our society. We need to create more open pathways to a design education, so that we can have a more inclusive way of solving the challenges we face. We have been focused on this for some time in our firm, and the only way to succeed at changing this balance is to keep trying. I just feel like the whole world is finally having this aha moment, and it is important to keep making progress toward change.

KLEIN: We must get more diverse voices into our field. The more our teams can look like and relate to the communities for which they are designing, the better the outcome will be. People are becoming more interested in improving the neighborhoods and the communities and cities in which they live, that impact them and their families. And our profession gives them a very real chance to effect positive change.

THOMÉ: Right. The challenges require collaboration with many voices and many disciplines. We are working hard to keep training our team on tools to foster this kind of cross-inquiry. We will continue to grow technology-wise. We can never get comfortable with a certain process or a way that we're doing something, because as soon as you get comfortable, you're not open to evolving and growing. I've already experienced so much just in fifteen years. It blows my mind to think of where we'll be in thirty more.

BURNETT: I hope that in thirty years, we will be looking at landscape with a new lens. It may not be called landscape architecture. It might be called environmental design or environmental architecture, because we are so much more than landscape. We know that our systems and networks are connected, and we need to be thinking in terms of the impact that we can have on our whole environment. I see our profession as being right in the middle of this conversation.

Science and technology are important tools, but landscape is science and art together. We are artists who are using a different palette to paint, and we want to make something beautiful and enduring to share. And, of course, I hope that there will always be those moments of magic and joy for everyone, sitting in the sunshine, smelling the perfume of a garden after a late summer rain.

The Burbank Studios,
Burbank, California

New
Perspectives

Mass General
Brigham Campus

Somerville, Massachusetts

On a new corporate campus, native and adaptive planting sequesters nearly forty thousand pounds of carbon annually.

This new campus of the Mass General Brigham administrative headquarters assembles nearly 4,500 employees of one of the region's largest health care systems. To realize a corporate campus in a newly developed, high-density district of Greater Boston, the project includes programmed spaces for both private and public use, which together form a benchmark for workplace design and sustainable practices

Private and semiprivate courtyards adjacent to the building are designed to follow a grid established by the architecture, promoting inside-outside connections. On the southeast side of the building, a 28,000-square-foot intensive-extensive green roof, which supports a private dining terrace, is shaded by nearly one hundred whitespire birch trees. These trees act as a curtain between two environments: on one side, the dining area is a clear extension of the interior, but just forty feet away, the trees create an intimate alcove. Precisely sloped planters extend from the dining area into the alcove, where they rise to a height that supports seating.

By contrast, a 2.5-acre publicly accessible event lawn is more free-form, featuring groves of river birch, maple, ginkgo, and redwood and a winding lawn trail that encourages guests of the campus to wander and spend time outdoors. The lawn bowl collects and stores water temporarily and a system of dry creekways directs stormwater out and away from the building. Native New England prairie planting and adaptive planting, including 133 trees, work together as a biofiltration system. Together they combat wind and transit noise and, more significantly, sequester nearly forty thousand pounds of carbon annually.

← The evolving workplace blurs the boundaries between indoors and out. The roof terrace expands the variety of places for collaboration and also supports special events, meetings, and informal gathering. → On the ground level, sustainable hardware such as bioswales and dry creeks is highlighted as a design feature, with walking paths purposely integrated into these natural systems.

↑ 23 September | 5:16 p.m.

← Formally gridded courtyards facilitate clear
indoor-outdoor connections, while winding
paths and groves of trees immerse guests in
nature, all within the same campus.

↑ 2 October | 5:43 p.m

→ The dry creek is structured by homogeneous New
England stones at the plaza and becomes more
organic and free-flowing as it enters the prairie.

→ 23 September | 5:54 p.m.

← A meandering fitness trail loops around the event lawn and guides guests on a journey through groves of maple, ginkgo, and redwood.

1. Garage
2. Retail streetscape
3. Entry drive
4. Transit connection
5. Shared-use path

6. Portal
7. Formal court
8. Bioretention cell
9. Dry creek
10. Event lawn

11. Stage
12. Roof terrace
13. Green roof
14. Fitness loop
15. Native prairie planting

Plantings

TREES

Acer × freemanii 'Autumn Blaze', Autumn Blaze maple

Acer rubrum 'Armstrong', Armstrong maple

Acer rubrum 'Red Sunset', Red Sunset maple

Betula papyrifera, paper birch

Carpinus betulus, European hornbeam

Ginkgo biloba, ginkgo

Gleditsia triacanthos var. *inermis* 'Skyline', Skyline honey locust

Metasequoia glyptostroboides, dawn redwood

Pinus strobus, eastern white pine

Platanus × Acerifolia, London plane

Quercus coccinea, scarlet oak

Quercus rubra, northern red oak

Ulmus americana 'Princeton', Princeton elm

SHRUBS & PERENNIALS

Aronia arbutifolia, red chokeberry

Chasmanthium latifolium, northern sea oats

Cornus sericea, red twig dogwood

Cornus sericea 'Kelseyi', dwarf red-twig dogwood

Forsythia × intermedia 'Beatrix Farrand', border forsythia

Hakonechloa macra 'All Gold', Hakone grass

Iris 'Caesar's Brother', Siberian iris

Ilex glabra 'Compacta', compact inkberry holly

Ilex verticillata, winterberry

Juniperus chinensis 'Sea Green', Sea Green juniper

Liriope gigantea, giant lilyturf

Liriope muscari 'Big Blue', Big Blue lilyturf

Myrica gale, sweet gale

Pachysandra terminalis, Japanese pachysandra

Pennisetum alopecuroides 'Hameln', Hameln fountain grass

Perovskia atriplicifolia 'Little Spire', Russian sage

Schizachyrium scoparium, little bluestem

CONSERVATION WILDLIFE MIX

Agrostis perennans, upland bentgrass

Andropogon gerardii, big bluestem

Asclepias tuberosa, butterfly milkweed

Aster pilosus/Symphyotrichum pilosum, frost aster

Chamaecrista fasciculata, partridge pea

Desmodium paniculatum, panicledleaf tick trefoil

Festuca rubra, red fescue

Helenium autumnale, common sneezeweed

Panicum virgatum, switchgrass

Rudbeckia hirta, black-eyed Susan

Schizachyrium scoparium, little bluestem

Sorghastrum nutans, Indian grass

Solidago juncea, early goldenrod

Verbena hastata, blue vervain

NEW ENGLAND WETLAND MIX

Asclepias incarnata, swamp milkweed

Aster puniceus, swamp aster

Bidens aristosa, tickseed sunflower/bur marigold

Carex crinita, fringed sedge

Carex lupulina, hop sedge

Carex lurida, lurid sedge

Carex vulpinoidea, fox sedge

Carex scoparia, blunt broom sedge

Eleocharis palustris, creeping spikerush

Eupatorium maculatum, spotted joe-pye weed

Glyceria canadensis, rattlesnake grass

Iris versicolor, blue flag

Juncus effusus, soft rush

Mimulus ringens, square-stemmed monkey flower

Poa palustris, fowl bluegrass

Scirpus atrovirens, green bulrush

Verbena hastata, blue vervain

WARM SEASON GRASS MIX

Andropogon gerardii, big bluestem

Elymus virginicus, Virginia wild rye

Festuca rubra, red fescue

Panicum virgatum, switchgrass

Schizachyrium scoparium, little bluestem

Sorghastrum nutans, Indian grass

Sustainability

LAND

History of former industrial site recognized while remediating degraded zones

Ecological conditions along Mystic River restored and floodplain function protected by design

WATER

1.8 acres of permeable surface created

Flood resilience promoted through stormwater features functioning as amenities, including bioswales, rain gardens, and detention ponds, and land mitigation strategies zoning portions of the site to accommodate flooding

28,000-square-foot green roof reduces heat island effect and absorbs stormwater

166,500 gallons of water—equivalent to the daily water usage of 1,665 Americans—can be intercepted annually by trees*

Water usage reduced through low-water planting

PLANTING

333 trees planted

Fertilizer and pesticide use minimized

Increased water and nutrient absorption by planting promoted through mycorrhizal fungi implemented in soil mix; carbohydrates for fungi provided, in turn, by planting

Plants allowed to go from seed to flower

Annual planting avoided

CARBON, ENERGY & AIR

Building energy use minimized by planting

Regional material utilized, reducing emissions resulting from transportation

Carbon emissions reduced by encouraging employees and visitors to utilize public transportation and bicycles

39,960 pounds of carbon—equivalent to the emissions produced by 4.8 passenger vehicles—sequestered annually by trees**

WASTE

Salvaged materials used

SOCIAL

Optimal site accessibility, safety, and wayfinding achieved through design

Extends retail experience of adjacent Assembly Row and culminates in a public amenity, the park

Site connects to bike trails along Mystic River and Sylvester Baxter Riverfront Park via multiuse path, encouraging public entry

4,300 employees relocated to the site, activing the surrounding area

Educational programs promoting sustainability hosted on-site

Rice University

Houston, Texas

The desire to create opportunities for gathering outside of the classroom, particularly in the landscape, has driven change.

Over a period of fifteen years, Rice University has sought to create more places for interaction and discovery, in both buildings and landscape spaces. With a small intervention—the addition of the Brochstein Pavilion—the university's central quadrangle has been reimagined as its social center. Although the six-thousand-square-foot pavilion is modest in size, it is activated and expanded by a ten- thousand-square-foot outdoor terrace that works synergistically as a campus hub. A grove of forty-eight lacebark elms, set in a field of decomposed granite, responds to the grid of the pavilion and organizes the area between the building and the adjacent Fondren Library. Two low concrete fountains define the space under the tree canopy, and movable seating accommodates impromptu gatherings of students and faculty. Additional plantings of live oaks and improved pedestrian paths reinforce the existing framework of the quadrangle.

As buildings were added to the campus, the desire to create opportunities for gathering outside of the classroom, particularly in the landscape, has driven change. The space under Brockman Hall for Physics, an 111,000-square-foot facility raised a full story above the ground on great concrete pilotis, provided an ideal area to forge an outdoor meeting place that was closely connected into the building. Housing classrooms, laboratory space, lecture halls, and administrative offices for the Department of Physics and Astronomy and physicists from the Department of Electrical and Computer Engineering, Brockman Hall brings the disciplines together; its ground-floor courtyard was conceived as a calm and comfortable backdrop for promoting connection and fostering dialogue. Sheltered from the sun by the building overhead, the courtyard features a reflecting pool, a raised ipe terrace, and an enhanced plaza with movable furniture.

Seeking to make the most of all interstitial spaces and expanding the visual language of landscape across campus, other quadrangles and courts utilize a spare vocabulary of water and stone, with branching trees that offer soft canopies across lawns and pathways.

Brochstein Pavilion

Planned as part of a larger vision to return the center of campus to a social hub, the serene spaces of the Brochstein Pavilion provide respite and invite relaxation. An allée of lacebark elms, together with linear fountains and comfortable seating, creates an oasis for gathering.

Brockman Hall for Physics

Brockman Hall for Physics is located at
the center of the engineering quadrangle
and its open spaces are a keystone in
the composition of informal gathering
areas, which are so important to scientific
dialogue and discovery.

↑ 10 March | 5:15 p.m.

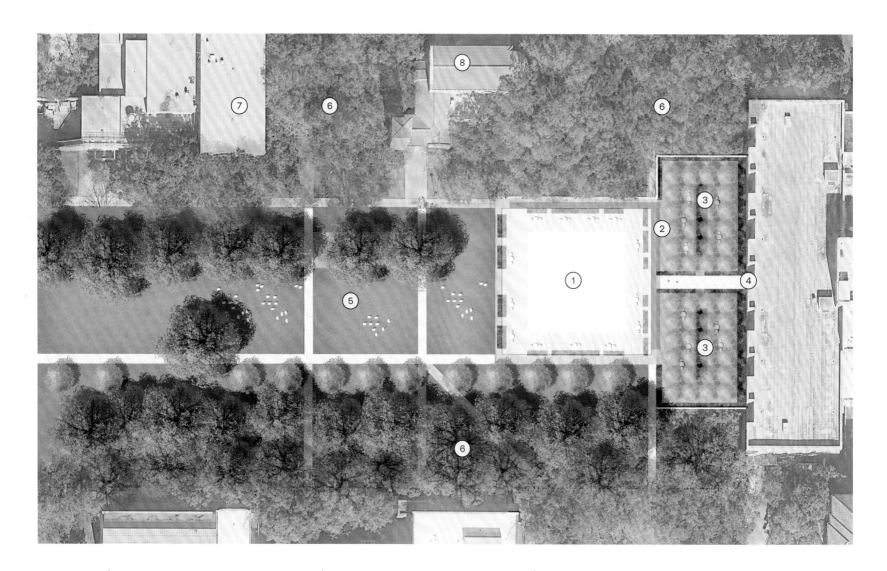

1. Brochstein Pavilion
2. Crownover Courtyard
3. Water feature
4. Fondren Library entry

5. Event lawn
6. Heritage oaks
7. Rice Memorial Center
8. Rice Memorial Chapel

Not shown:
Brockman Hall for Physics

Plantings

TREES

Quercus virginiana, live oak

Ulmus crassifolia, cedar elm

Ulmus parvifolia 'Emer II' ALLEE, lacebark elm

SHRUBS & PERENNIALS

Cephalotaxus harringtonia, plum yew

Dietes iridioides, African iris

Equisetum spp., horsetail

Ophiopogon japonicus 'Nanus', dwarf mondo grass

Trachelospermum asiaticum, Asian jasmine

Schizachyrium scoparium, little bluestem

LAWN

Cynodon dactylon × C. *transvaalensis*, Tifway Bermuda grass

Stenotaphrum secundatum, St. Augustine grass

Sustainability

LAND

Historic context considered and architecture of campus united by landscape

Healthy soils conserved

14,000 square feet of landscaped open space added to campus and floodplain function of site protected by Brockman design, which lifts building above the ground and allows for landscape amenity below

WATER

8,000 gallons of water—equivalent to daily water usage of 800 Americans—can be intercepted by trees*

56 inches of rain intercepted by trees annually, exceeding average annual rainfall of 49.6 inches

56% of surfaces permeable

PLANTING

Vegetation conserved when appropriate

Annual planting avoided

91 trees preserved and 69 trees planted on Brochstein site

17 trees planted on Brockman site

CARBON, ENERGY & AIR

Reduction in temperature of outdoor spaces by fountains

Regional material utilized, reducing emissions resulting from transportation

Light pollution reduced by use of full cutoff fixtures on Brochstein site

19,200 pounds of carbon—equivalent to emissions produced by driving 2.3 passenger vehicles—sequestered annually by trees on Brochstein site**

SOCIAL

Optimal site accessibility, safety, and wayfinding achieved through design

New location for social gatherings, research groups, and campus meetings provided by pavilion

Academic classes, outdoor fitness programs, and educational tours take place in landscape

WASTE

Reusable vegetation, rocks, and soil are diverted from disposal

ACKNOWLEDGMENTS

For centuries, humans have written about the mutability and power of nature—how a landscape transforms with every successive season and the fragility of its composition, how we change when we are in nature, and how even small gestures can make our environment better.

These many influences of nature are heightened and pronounced as I reflect on more than thirty years of practice in landscape architecture. The collection of projects in this book is a small sample of this exploration, but represents a diverse approach to how people can connect and communicate with one another and within the environment. Landscapes are a democratic and a shared experience, and they can restore and transform us.

I am honored and humbled to have shared the creative process with a talented and dedicated group of collaborators. These collaborations are also mutable and always transforming. I am grateful to my partners who have a mutual vision for the impact and promise of landscape, and for their energy and their individual voices, which have shaped the journey along the way. We have striven to create places that delight the senses and bring people together.

I am grateful to Christa Mahar and our creative team at OJB who have helped collect and present the material for these projects, as well as assisted in the task of marrying words with images. We are also in debt to our editor at Monacelli, Jenny Florence, for her keen guidance and support. Blake Goodwin, Paul Reiss, and Megan Le at Proportion have created an elegant structure in which to present the work. And perhaps the most meaningful contributions have come from the fellow practitioners who have shaped the profession in profound and different ways: Peter Walker, one of my first mentors and a landscape architect who has produced a catalogue of work that is unmatched in contemporary practice; Christopher Hawthorne, a journalist, teacher, and thinker who is shaping the future of our cities in a wholly new way; and Brad McKee, a design journalist who has elevated landscape architecture into the public discourse.

Finally, I want to thank my wife, Kim, who never doubted me during this more than thirty-year journey of late nights and weekly trips, as well as my sons, Cameron and Kendall. Your support has given me the confidence to continually explore new directions and opportunities.

James Burnett, FASLA

CONTRIBUTORS

Christopher Hawthorne

Christopher Hawthorne is chief design officer for the City of Los Angeles, a position appointed by Mayor Eric Garcetti. In that capacity he focuses on projects related to urban planning, public art, architecture, and the design of the public realm. Prior to joining City Hall, he was the architecture critic for the *Los Angeles Times* from 2004 to 2018. His writing has also appeared in the *New York Times*, the *New Yorker*, the *Washington Post*, Slate, *Harvard Design Magazine*, and many other publications. He is professor of the practice at the University of Southern California's Dornsife College of Letters, Arts and Sciences, where he directs the Third Los Angeles Project, a series of public conversations about architecture, urban planning, mobility, and demographic change in Southern California.

Bradford McKee

Bradford McKee was the editor of *Landscape Architecture Magazine* from 2010 to 2020. Upon joining the magazine during its hundredth year, he redesigned and relaunched the title to position landscape architecture as the natural lead discipline among the environmental design fields for an era of repair around climate change, spatial justice, and ecological health, and with an emphasis on the inherent adventure of landscape design. The magazine received numerous awards during his tenure and, in 2014, *LAM* was named as a National Magazine Award finalist for general excellence. Before joining *LAM*, McKee was a senior editor and later an editor at large at the magazine *Architecture*, the arts editor of the weekly *Washington City Paper*, and a contract reporter for the *New York Times*. He has written and edited features for numerous magazines, and is the author of three books on architecture and landscape architecture.

Peter Walker, FASLA

Over his five-decade career, Peter Walker has exerted a significant influence on the field of landscape architecture. Educated at the University of California at Berkeley and the Harvard University Graduate School of Design, Walker has taught at, lectured at, written for, and served as an advisor to numerous public agencies. His projects range from small gardens to new cities, from urban plazas to corporate headquarters and academic campuses, all with a dedicated concern for urban and environmental issues, in a variety of geographic and cultural contexts, from the United States to Japan, China, Australia, and Europe. Walker is a Fellow of the American Society of Landscape Architects and of the Institute for Urban Design and, in addition to numerous awards for specific projects, has been granted the Honor Award of the American Institute of Architects, Harvard's Centennial Medal, the University of Virginia's Thomas Jefferson Medal, the American Society of Landscape Architects Medal, and the International Federation of Landscape Architects Sir Geoffrey Jellicoe Gold Medal.

Northwestern Mutual Headquarters,
Milwaukee, Wisconsin

TEAM

Partners

James Burnett (1989)

Chip Trageser (1997)

Jereck Boss (1998)

Kyle Fiddelke (1998)

Meg Levy (2003)

Claudia Thomé (2005)

Dillon Diers (2006)

Cody Klein (2011)

Bold denotes active team member at time of publication

Team

Eliana Abu-Hamdi

Andrew Albers

Cindy Alfaro

Ernesto Alfaro

Colby Alston

Corianne Andrews

Brandon Barrera

Simon Beer

Taffie Behringer

Mari Bendinsky

Ted Benge

William Benge

Amy Benoit

Matthew Biesecker

Brittany Blicharz

Scott Blons

Prajakti Bokil

Alexandra Bolinder-Gibsand

Isabella Boss

Brian Boyd

Tarah Brand

Darby Buckley

Michael Bullis

Kinsey Burdette

Maricela Burke

Patti Caldwell

Ben Canales

Georgie Cantu

Jeanette Cantu

Madison Cao

Rafael Carbajal

Paul Carcamo

Suzanne Carr

Jessie Carvajal

Nate Carvin

Charlie Cattlett

Meredith Chavez

Lingya Chen

Charity Cheung

Danielle Collins

Troy Cook

David Cooley

Andrew Cridlin

Adrianne Cruz

Lisa Davis

Cynthia Dehlavi

Leigha DelBusso

Kelly Dendy

Erin Dibos

Brian Dickson

Brittany Dixon

Linh Do

Ned Dodington

Ally Dougherty

Christina Drury

Lina Duong

Paul Dupnik

Nathan Elliott

Allison Walling Ellis

Courtney Emerson

Marcus Farr

Jonathan Fedee

Jason Ferster

Marcus Fiedler

Amanda Foran

Micki Forsyth

Cristina Frass

Brian Frederick

Amanda Furr

Jennifer Gaines

Federico Garcia- Anquiano

Randall Gay

Rocio Gertler

Ramon Gisbert

Ben Granovsky

Stephanie Green

Tara Green

Jeff Grossman

Ryan Harbert

Ryan Harrison

Michelle Hartmann

Bill Hartmon

Allison Harvey

Jun Hashimoto

Josh Hellewell

Kevin Henn

Sam Heritage

Caroline Hickey

Drew Hill

Rita Hodge

Ingrid Imechaley

Jennifer Irwin

Taran Jensvold

Cheryl Johnson

Gabriel Juarez

Tyler Jurney

Megan Kemp

Hyun Kim

Jungsoo Kim

Thomas King

Bryan Leavitt

Caroline Lezon

Bernard Lighter

Seaton Lin

Yisi Liu

Yuting Liu

Kimberly Lombardino

Victoria Lorenz

Cheryl Lough

Connie Lu

Alexandra Ludas

Nabyl Macias

Matt MacLeod

Christa Mahar

Lesley Ann Malapit

Shannon Marquardt

Jeremy Martin

Lalise Mason

Maria Mateo-Castro

John McBride

Michelle McCloskey

Maggie McCullough

Connor McInerney

Rebecca McKevitz

Cynthia McMillioan

Eric McWilliam

Rich Melcher

Brad Meyerhoff

Olivia Miethke

Marissa Mijal

Ana Millan

Andrew Miller

Suzy Minor

Hannah Moll

Daniel Monti

Brendan Mulcahy

A. John Musser

Alexander Nagel

Doan Nguyen

Huong (Debe) Nguyen

Katie Nguyen

Chandler Nohr

David Norgard

Aron Nussbaum

Kezia Ofiesh

Alexis Opos

Shayna Orr

Ryan Ort

Jamin Pablo

Charlie Palanza

Shi Park

Thomas Parker

Cyndy Parnell

Samantha Partington

Sean Passler

Frank Pavon

Lana Peralta

Mark Petterson

Kevin Pfeiffer

Steven Piper

Anne Plowden

Max Polonchak

Juan Prieto

Eric Pullen

Jessy Qiu

Angela Quintanilla

Jesse Quintanilla

Theresa Quintanilla

Babak Rastkar

Juliane Roberts

Sarah Rogers

Kay Ross

Gitte Russo

Joanna Sabra

Zachary Sawchuk

Emily Scarfe

Ryan Scharlemann

Brendan Schartz

John Schroeder

Karli Scott

Justin Seale

Matt Shearer

Xiwei Shen

Chris Shern

Judy Shern

Sookyung Shin

Jamar Simien

Rachel Sloan

Shelly Smith

Aaron Spell

Sheridan Staats

Casey Stallcup

Drew Stangel

Sarah Nitchman Stangel

Ryan Steib

August Stone

Terry Stone

Biff Sturgess

Shane Sullivan

Jianing Tao

Andrew Taylor

Brice Tegeler

Mallory Thomas

Cindy Tong

Gabriela Toriello

Sara Tyler

Troy Vaughn

Garrett Vinyard

Sara Vissering

Amanda Walker

Abbey Wallace

Mary Moore Wallinger

Yangdi Wang

Yiqing Wang

Chase Weaver

Steve Weber

Linda West

Rachel Wilkins

Seong-Hyeak Won

Jay Woodard

Yiting Xi

Feng Xu

Tianjiao Ye

Patricio Yrizar

Rosa Zedek

Xiao Zhou

PROJECT DATA

Hall Winery

2014

Client: Hall Wines

St. Helena, California

35 acres

Shade trees, perennial plantings, signature sculpture, auto court, event lawn, gravel terrace, limestone walls, cutting garden, kitchen garden, olive grove

Architect: Signum Architecture

Civil Engineer: Summit Engineering

Structural Engineer: Buro Happold

MEP Engineer: TEP Engineering

Irrigation: Sweeney & Associates

Lighting: HLB Lighting Design

Water Feature Consultant: Fluidity Design Consultants

Interior Design: Nicole Hollis Designs

Klyde Warren Park

2012

Client: Woodall Rodgers Park Foundation

Dallas, Texas

5.2 acres

Promenade, botanical garden, children's garden, interactive water features, reading room, event lawn, public plaza, restaurant terrace, performance pavilion, takeout pavilion

Architect: Thomas Phifer and Partners

Civil Engineer: Jacobs Engineering Group

Structural Engineer: Jacobs Engineering Group, Thornton Tomasetti

Irrigation: Sweeney & Associates

Lighting: Focus Lighting

Water Feature Consultant: Fluidity Design Consultants

Activation Planning: Biederman Redevelopment Ventures

Signage & Wayfinding: Thomas Phifer and Partners, Focus EGD

Park Installations Architect: Endrc studio

Levy Park

2017

Client: Upper Kirby Redevelopment Authority

Houston, Texas

5.9 acres

Activity lawn, gaming area, shade arbor, event pavilion, children's garden, interactive sculptures and fountains, tree house, reading room, dog play areas, community garden, promenade

Architect: Natalye Appel + Associates

Civil Engineer: WGA Consulting Engineers

Structural Engineer: Matrix Structural Engineers

MEP Engineer: Wylie Engineering

Irrigation: Ellis Glueck

Water Feature Consultant: Fountain Source

Activation Planning: Biederman Redevelopment Ventures

Signage & Wayfinding: Minor Design

Security: 4b Technology

Mass General Brigham Campus

2018

Client: Mass General Brigham

Somerville, Massachusetts

10 acres

Private and semiprivate courtyards, event lawn, shade groves, fitness loop, green roof, native planting

Architect: Gensler

Civil Engineer: Vanasse Hangen Brustlin, Inc.

Structural Engineer: McNamara Salvia

MEP Engineer: Buro Happold

Environmental & Geotechnical Engineer: Haley & Aldrich

Lighting: HLB Lighting Design

Landscape Consultant: Ryan Associates

Oklahoma City Renaissance

Devon Energy Headquarters

2012

Client: Devon Energy Corporation

Oklahoma City, Oklahoma

2.25 acres

Design Architect: Pickard Chilton

Architect of Record: Kendall/Heaton Associates

Civil Engineer: Smith Roberts Baldischwiler

Structural Engineer: Thornton Tomasetti

MEP Engineer: Cosentini Associates

Irrigation: Murase Associates

Lighting: Quentin Thomas Associates

Water Feature Consultant: Fluidity Design Consultants

Landscape Consultant: Murase Associates

Interior Architect: Gensler

Security: HMA Consulting

Myriad Botanical Gardens

2011

Client: City of Oklahoma City

Oklahoma City, Oklahoma

15 acres

Tree-lined promenade, botanical plantings, shaded berms, sculptural band shell, sycamore grove, interactive water feature, children's garden, dog park, fountain plaza, restaurant terrace, event lawn

Architect: Gensler, Frankfurt Short Bruza

Civil Engineer: Cardinal Engineering

Structural Engineer: Thornton Tomasetti

MEP Engineer: Alvine Engineering

Irrigation: Sweeney & Associates

Lighting: Fisher Marantz Stone

Water Feature Consultant: Fluidity Design Consultants, Pacific Aquascape

Signage & Wayfinding: Dyal and Partners

Associate Landscape Architect: Murase Associates

Arborist: Robert Birchell & Associates

Horticulturists: Mike Schnelle, PhD, Mary Irish

Sunshades & Decks Engineer: Endrestudio

Streetscape 180

2017

Client: City of Oklahoma City

Oklahoma City, Oklahoma

180 acres

Civil Engineers: Cardinal Engineering, Coon Engineering, Legacy Engineering, Lemke Land Surveying, MacArthur Associated Consultants, Myers Engineering, Smith Roberts Baldischwiler

Consultant Team: Murase Associates, Jeff Speck & Associates, Howard-Fairbairn Site Design, Carter Design Group, CLS & Associates, Robert Lewis & Associates, Tetra Tech Traffic Engineering Consultants, White Engineering, LiFang International

The Park at Lakeshore East

2005

Client: Lakeshore East LLC, City of Chicago, Magellan Development Group

Chicago, Illinois

5.3 acres

Tree-lined promenades, fountain basins, flexible seating, ornamental gardens, grand stair, children's garden, dog park, event lawn

Architect: SOM

Landscape Architect of Record: Site Design Group

Playa Vista

Central Park

2011

Client: Playa Vista Capital

Playa Vista, California

9 acres

Sports courts, soccer field, playground, botanical gardens, water features, lawn, performance pavilion

Architect:
Michael Maltzan Architecture

Civil Engineer: Psomas

Structural Engineer: Arup

Site Electrical Engineer: West Coast Design Group

Irrigation: Sweeney & Associates

Lighting: HLB Lighting Design

Signage & Wayfinding:
Biesek Design

Lake Engineer: Pacific Aquascape

The Campus at Playa Vista

2010

Client: Tishman Speyer

Playa Vista, California

6.9 acres

Office development with structured parking, terraces atop garage deck, event lawns, seating areas

Architect: Gensler

Civil Engineer: Psomas

Structural Engineer:
Nabih Youssef Associates

Irrigation: Sweeney & Associates

Lighting: HLB Lighting Design

Signage & Wayfinding: Gensler

The Collective

2016

Client: Tishman Speyer

Playa Vista, California

6.3 acres

Five-building commercial campus, welcome court, event lawn, private gravel seating patios, shade tree allées, shared courtyards, sculptural seating berms, native ornamental planting

Architect: Shimoda Design Group

Civil Engineer: Psomas

Irrigation: Sweeney & Associates

Randy Johnson Bluff Creek Fields

2015

Client: Brookfield Residential

Playa Vista, California

3.5 acres

Soccer field, tennis courts, grass play area, playgrounds, event spaces, dog park for small breeds, dog park for large breeds

Architect: Endrestudio

Civil Engineer: Psomas

Irrigation: Sweeney & Associates

Rice University

Brochstein Pavilion

2008

Client: Rice University

Houston, Texas

5.14 acres

Refreshments pavilion, covered terrace, decomposed granite plaza, shade grove, fountain basins, flexible seating

Architect: Thomas Phifer and Partners

Civil Engineer: Ulrich Engineers, Inc.

Structural Engineer: Walter P Moore, Haynes Whaley Associates

MEP Engineer: Altieri Sebor Wieber

Lighting: Fisher Marantz Stone

Brockman Hall for Physics

2011

Client: Rice University

Houston, Texas

3.25 acres

Reflecting pool, raised wood terrace, hardscape plaza, flexible furniture, shade grove, decomposed granite plaza

Architect: KieranTimberlake

Civil Engineer: Walter P Moore

Structural Engineer: Haynes Whaley Associates

MEP Engineer: CCRD Partners

Lighting: Arup

Geotechnical Engineering:
Ulrich Engineers, Inc.

Sunnylands Center and Gardens

2011

Client: Annenberg Foundation Trust at Sunnylands

Rancho Mirage, California

15 acres

Interpretive center, theater, gift shop, event terrace, event lawn, reflecting basins, labyrinth, native plants

Architect: Frederick Fisher and Partners

Civil Engineer:
MSA Engineering Consultants

Structural Engineer:
Leo Parker Engineering

MEP Engineer: G&W Engineering

Irrigation: Sweeney & Associates

Lighting: HLB Lighting Design

Water Feature Consultant:
CMS Collaborative

Exhibit Design: Hillmann & Carr

Signage & Wayfinding:
Reich&Petch

IMAGE CREDITS

Alonzo Adams
62–63

Sibylle Allgaier/Heliphoto.net
138, 141, 149, 155

Caitlin Atkinson/The Annenberg
Foundation Trust at Sunnylands
4–5, 154, 157

Craig Blackmon
230–31

Michael Brands/The Annenberg
Foundation Trust at Sunnylands
147, 152

Marion Brenner
2, 14, 26, 32, 34, 66, 69, 72–73, 78–81,
86, 106–8, 116, 118–20, 125–26, 128,
150–51, 153, 156, 160, 164, 168, 172,
181, 185

Kyle J. Caldwell
6, 188–201, 204

Serhii Chrucky
96, 104

David Cobb
70–71, 82, 84–85, 87, 92

John D'Angelo
179

Devon Energy Corporation
83

Dillon Diers Photography
18–19, 110–12, 114, 121, 144–46, 148,
174, 222

Jeff Durkin
136–37, 140

Nathan Elliot
166

Andrew G.
64

Hall Wines
162–63

Hester + Hardaway
113, 115, 117, 132, 206, 208–10, 212–15,
218

Ken Hayden
142–43

Mei-Chun Jau
28–30

Geoff Lyon
44–46, 50–54, 56–57, 60

Bryan Malloch
40–41, 47–49

Duncan Martin
8, 12

Thomas McConnell
20

Zach Nash
74

OJB Landscape Architecture
101

Thomas Orellana
55

Prakash Patel
68, 75–77

Ian Patzke
224

Undine Prohl
122–24, 127

Mitch Rice
167

Rocket Brand
22–23, 35

Zachary Sawchuck
129

David Seide
99

Carl Shortt
67

Slyworks Photography
182

Steinkamp Photography
94–95, 98, 100

Trey Stephens/
alwayslookdown
42

David Sundberg/Esto
220–21

Liane Swanson
24, 27, 31

Chip Trageser
169

Payne Wingate
10, 25

Gary Zvonkovic
33

Library of Congress Control Number: 2021931773

ISBN 978-1-58093-567-8

Printed in China

Design by Proportion

Monacelli
A Phaidon Company
65 Bleecker Street
New York, NY 10012
monacellipress.com

Cover: Sibylle Allgaier/Heliphoto.net
Back cover: Dillon Diers Photography

*The tree average for water interception is 500
gallons; Americans use an average of 100 gallons
of water per day (EPA)

** 120 pounds of carbon per tree annually
(based on an average from National Tree Benefits
Calculator , Casey Trees); one car produces an
average of 8,320 pounds of CO2 per year (The
Code of Federal Regulations - 40 CFR 600.113)